CITIES IN OUR FUTURE

CITIES
IN
OUR FUTURE

Growth and Form

Environmental Health and Social Equity

Edited by Robert Geddes

ISLAND PRESS
Washington, D.C. ● Covelo, California

Copyright © 1997 by Island Press

All rights reserved under International and Pan-American Copyright Conventions. No part of this book may be reproduced in any form or by any means without permission in writing from the publisher: Island Press, 1718 Connecticut Avenue, N.W., Suite 300, Washington, DC 20009.

ISLAND PRESS is a trademark of The Center for Resource Economics.

Library of Congress Cataloging-in-Publication Data

Cities in our future / edited by Robert Geddes.
     p.   cm.
    "Based on the Conference on Cities in North America (CCNA) held in New York in 1996"—Pref.
    Includes bibliographical references and index.
    ISBN 1-55963-496-0 (cloth)
    1. Cities and towns—North America—Growth. 2. Cities and towns—North America—Case studies. 3. Urbanization—North America. 4. City planning—North America. I. Geddes, Robert. II. Conference on Cities in North America (1996 : New York, N.Y.)
HT384.N5C57 1997
307.76'0973—dc20   96-31797
                                                             CIP

Printed on recycled, acid-free paper ♻

Manufactured in the United States of America

10 9 8 7 6 5 4 3 2 1

Contents

New York City and the New York Region

Cascadia: Portland, Seattle, and Vancouver

Mexico City and Its Region

Contributors

═══

ALAN ARTIBISE is a professor in the School of Community and Regional Planning, University of British Columbia, Vancouver. He is the founding executive director of the International Centre for Sustainable Cities and the president of Cascadia Planning Group, specializing in urban and regional planning and working with communities in promoting sustainable development. He is the author of numerous books and articles on North American urban policy and has lectured extensively on urban growth and change in Canada, the United States, and more than 20 other countries. He has been a central figure in the development of the Cascadia concept since 1990.

JONATHAN BARNETT is an urban designer with a national practice and is a professor of architecture and director of the Graduate Program in Urban Design at City College of New York. He is the author of *Urban Design as Public Policy; Introduction to Urban Design; The Elusive City; Five Centuries of Design, Ambition, and Miscalculation;* and *The Fractured Metropolis: Improving the New City, Restoring the Old City, Reshaping the Region.*

ALIYE PEKIN CELIK is the officer-in-charge of the New York office of the United Nations Centre for Human Settlements. She has been a researcher and lecturer for the Scientific and Technical Research Council of Turkey's Building Research Institute and has worked in the Building Infrastructure Technology Section of the UNCHS (Habitat) headquarters in Nairobi, Kenya. She has written numerous articles and books emphasizing the importance of affordable, appropriate housing, and energy planning and conservation, and she has received the American Institute of Architects Award for Excellence.

GARDNER CHURCH is associate professor of urban studies at York University and the University of Waterloo. He served 25 years as deputy minister and general policy advisor for the government of the province of Ontario in the field of housing and urban affairs. He has written and lectured extensively on urban affairs issues throughout Canada and the United States.

TIM FORD is an associate professor of environmental microbiology in the Department of Environmental Health at the Harvard School of Public Health and director of a new program in water and health. His publications include *Aquatic Microbiology: An Ecological Approach* (editor), and an American Academy of Microbiology report entitled "A Global Decline in Microbiological Safety of Water: A Call for Action" (co-coordinator).

ROBERT GEDDES is an architect and urban designer. He was dean of the School of Architecture at Princeton University for 17 years. In 1990 he became the Luce Professor of Architecture, Urbanism and History at New York University, and a fellow of New York Institute for the Humanities at New York University. He received the AIA/ACSA Education Medal and the AIA Professional Firm Award for excellence in design. His works include the Institute for Advanced Study, Princeton; Liberty State Park in New York Harbor; the Center City Plan of Philadelphia; and the Manhattan Crosstown concept for the Regional Plan Association.

KENNETH GREENBERG is an architect and urban designer. He was the founder and director of the Division of Architecture and Urban Design in Toronto's Department of Planning and Development. He is currently an advisor to the Waterfront Regeneration Trust and has served on an international advisory committee concerning the Amsterdam waterfront. With French architect Antoine Gumbach, he won a competition for a new community in the Saclay Region outside Paris. His projects include the campus plans for the University of Minnesota in Minneapolis–St. Paul and they have earned his firm numerous awards, including the 1994 Toronto Arts Award for Architecture and Design.

FERNANDO GREENE is an architect with a master's degree in urbanism from the Universidad Nacional Autonoma de Mexico (UNAM) and a Ph.D. in planning from Cornell University. From 1990 to 1994 he served as chair of the Graduate Studies in Architecture program at UNAM. He was president of the Mexican Society of Planners from 1992 through 1995 and is currently a member of the Mexican Academy of Architects.

MARILOU MCPHEDRAN is an attorney and community advocate. She served as the head of Toronto's Healthy City Project from 1991 to 1994. She is now the volunteer president of the Metro Action Committee on Violence Against Women and Children and is the corporate director of Women's Health Partnerships at Women's College Hospital. She was installed as a member of the Order of Canada in recognition of her role in amending the Canadian constitution to strengthen women's equality rights.

ANNE VERNEZ MOUDON is professor of architecture, landscape architecture and urban design and planning at the University of Washington in Seattle, where she is also director of the Cascadia Community and Environment Institute. She has consulted nationally and internationally on developing urban design guidelines for new construction that respects the character of the existing landscape and built environment and that supports nonmotorized transportation. She is the author of *Built for Change: Neighborhood Architecture in San Francisco* and *Public Streets for Public Use.*

WALLY N'DOW is the secretary-general of the United Nations Centre for Human Settlements–Habitat II. He was instrumental in the formation of the International Fund for Agricultural Development and the World Food Council, and he has worked extensively with the Organization for Economic Co-operation and Development. He has also served as the United Nations regional director for Africa, UN Development Programme resident in the Central African Republic and Tanzania, and chief of the East Africa Division of the United Nations. He serves also as assistant secretary-general of the UN Centre for Human Settlements in Nairobi, Kenya.

ELLEN POSNER is an author and critic who writes about architecture and urban issues. She was the architecture and urbanism critic of the *Wall Street Journal* for 11 years and has published works in numerous publications, including *The Atlantic Monthly, ARTnews, The Independent* (London), and *Quaderno d'Arquitectura i Urbanisme* (Barcelona).

XAVIER CORTES ROCHA has been dean of the faculty of architecture at the Universidad Nacional Autonoma de Mexico since 1990 and has been a planning area professor there since 1968. He is coordinator of the Education/Experience subcommittee within the Tri-National Committee for Architect's Professional Education in Mexico, the United States, and Canada. His previous book projects include *Invasion on Urban Land, Manual for the Elaboration of Urban Plans* (author); *Six Years of Architecture in Mexico* (general coordinator); and *The Architecture of Ciudad Universitaria* (general coordinator). He is also a correspondent in Mexico for the French journal *Urbanisme.*

ALAN RYAN was a professor of politics at Princeton University and led the Program in Ethics and Public Affairs in the Center for Human Values. He is a fellow of the British Academy and for 20 years was a reader in politics at Oxford University. He recently returned to Oxford University to serve as warden of New College. He is the author of *Bertrand Russell: A Political Life* and *John Dewey and the High Tide of American Liberalism,* and the editor of *Justice.* He has also written, reviewed, and edited for the *New York Review of Books, The*

New York Times, the *New Republic,* and the *Times Literary Supplement,* among others, on issues ranging from the connections between race and intelligence to the shortcomings of economic theories of development.

ETHAN SELTZER is director of the Institute of Portland Metropolitan Studies at Portland State University in Portland, Oregon. He has also served as the land use supervisor for Metro, the regional government in the Portland area, and helped to develop its regional land use goals and objectives and its growth management program. He has received awards from the Oregon Chapter of the American Planning Association for his work in the Portland metropolitan area.

JOHN SPENGLER is professor of environmental health and director of the Environmental Science and Engineering Program of the Harvard School of Public Health. He served as principal investigator in the Harvard Six Cities Health Study on the respiratory health and air pollution exposure of children and adults in six U.S. communities. He also participates in exposure and health assessments in Germany, Austria, Mexico, Taiwan, China, Korea, and the Czech and Slovak Republics. He has served as an advisor to the World Health Organization on indoor air pollution, personal exposure, and air pollution epidemiology. Recently he served as a member of the National Academy of Science's Committee on Risk Assessment of Hazardous Air Pollutants. He is one of four authors of *Health Effects of Fossil Fuel Burning: Assessment and Mitigation,* and is co-editor and contributing author of *Indoor Air Pollution: A Health Perspective.*

RICHARD WEINSTEIN is an architect and urban designer. He is dean of the UCLA Graduate School of Architecture and Urban Planning, and president of his own design and consulting firm. He was vice-president of design and program development for the City at 42nd Street project and has also served as director of the Mayor's Office of Lower Manhattan Development and director of the New York City Department of Planning. He has done extensive consulting and design work and serves on numerous advisory boards, including as co-chair of Los Angeles's 2000 Partnership on Regional Governance and Environmental Management and as co-founder of the Los Angeles Mayor's Design Advisory Panel.

THOMAS K. WRIGHT is director of Regional Plan Association's Governance Campaign, one of the five major campaigns outlined in RPA's Third Regional Plan. He also provides support to RPA's other project teams by writing, editing, and managing research documents and publications. The RPA publications he has authored or co-authored include *A Region at Risk: The Third Regional Plan for the New York–New Jersey–Connecticut Metropolitan Area*; an Executive Summary of the Third Regional Plan; the 1995 and 1996 Quality of Life polls; *Downtown Brooklyn: A Plan for Continued Progress*; and RPA's *Declaration of Interdependence*, published in *The New York Times*.

ROBERT D. YARO is executive director of Regional Plan Association and has principal responsibility for preparing a new regional plan for the New York region. He has also served as chief planner and deputy commissioner of the Massachusetts Department of Environmental Management and as professor and director of the Graduate Program in Regional Planning at the University of Massachusetts, Amherst. He is the author of *Dealing with Change in the Connecticut River Valley*, which received awards from the National Trust for Historic Preservation and the National Planning Association. His most recent book is *A Region at Risk: The Third Regional Plan for the New York–New Jersey–Connecticut Metropolitan Area*.

Foreword

Urbanization is no longer a purely local dilemma. It is a phenomenon with distinctly international overtones, a reality not to be denied by any of us. Our common future hangs in the balance, and our task is to find a way to make what is happening sustainable and affordable. That calls for new and safer technology. It calls for creative and innovative management if we are to off-set the great danger inherent in the teeming, overcrowded cities and towns—indeed, human settlements of all sizes—that are now the hallmark of our new urban world.

Just take a walk in Washington Square Park, or just walk outside the United Nations on 42nd Street. Walk on the streets of Lagos, the streets of Paris, Tokyo, Bombay. The scars of urban life are all too evident; some places more, some places less. But be it homelessness, inadequate shelter, paralyz-ing gridlock, mounting crime, decaying infrastructure, or polluted air and water, it is everywhere. We are all in it together, North and South, East and West. We are all caught up in a historic and painful transition that has still to run its course. The world over, urbanization, and its fallout, is the common denominator of humanity.

Whether it is the consequence of a stream of rural–urban migration due to population growth and decreasing opportunities, a legacy of economic crises of past decades, or rapid economic change driven by infrastructure, the vast dimensions of the urban challenge now confronting us, the sheer number of people involved, especially in the developing countries—where the peril is intensified in the rapid growth of dehumanizing slums and shantytowns, most without adequate water or sanitation—is threatening to overwhelm the ability of authorities to cope with what has become one of the most com-pelling issues of our time.

Intensifying the risk is a looming environmental crisis. Just as it is true that the majority of the world's population will soon be living in overcrowded cities and towns, it is also true that it is in those same cities and towns, North and South, where most industrial pollution and emissions are being generated.

The problems resulting from unplanned urban growth increase in scope and intensity each day. What can be done? Governments can pass laws and provide resources that will implement these laws. But when all is said and done, it is the global community, the "global village" as Barbara Ward called it a generation ago, that must fulfill what we envisage. This can only happen if citizens take action.

We cannot just talk about our cities any longer, we have to act. If all that Habitat II did was decry the situation, we may as well not have gone to Istanbul. The job cannot be done just by cursing the darkness and telling the world what it already knows about its cities and the crises afflicting them.

The answer lies in taking on the responsibility—at the global, national, and municipal levels—to do what must be done if the new century is not to perpetuate the ills of the old. It lies in the willingness to take chances; to try new models of human settlements that rely on shared community responsibilities; it lies finally in the partnerships we require if society is to meet the needs we all share with our neighbors in this global village we call home.

WALLY N'DOW

Preface

≡

By its form, as by the manner of its birth, the city has elements at once of biological procreation, organic evolution and aesthetic creation. It is both a natural object and
a thing to be cultivated; something lived and something
dreamed.
It is the human invention par excellence.
Claude Levi-Strauss

What is happening to our cities, our landscapes, our human settlements?

That question was the key to the United Nations Conference on Human
Settlements, Habitat II. This was the last of a series of world conferences held
by the United Nations in the 1990s, starting with the *natural environment*
conference in Rio in 1992, and ending with Habitat II, the *built environment*
conference, in Istanbul in 1996.

Like Habitat I in Vancouver in 1976, the 1996 conference focused on
human life and how it is increasingly affected by the built environment. By
the year 2000, one-half of humanity will live and work in cities and towns;
and nearly everyone will rely on cities and towns for economic and environmental well-being, perhaps survival. The special challenge of Habitat II was
to come to grips with the explosive growth of the built environment.

The recommendations of the Habitat 1 conference were largely directed at
the needs and circumstances of developing countries, because it was taken
for granted that developed countries with ample resources and institutional
capabilities could meet all their human settlement needs in the normal course
of events. But now the problems of urbanization are everywhere; they are

global, national, regional, and local; public and private; long-term and immediate. There are lessons to be learned by everyone—in both developed and developing countries—if human settlements are to be livable in the future.

This is not a lesson book but rather a collection of perspectives. Based on the *Conference on Cities in North America* held in New York in 1996 to prepare for the Istanbul world conference, it is a critical self-analysis of cities in the United States, Canada, and Mexico. What have we learned about the planning and design, organization and governance, construction and preservation of our cities? What can we tell the rest of the world about improving the built environment?

The book is like a matrix. One part has thematic studies of social equity and environmental health that challenge the way we judge cities. The other part has contrasting studies of the growth and form of cities and regions.

The thematic studies analyze two fundamental issues that are embodied in the built environment. The issues—social equity and environmental health—affect us directly in our everyday lives, as individuals and as communities. But it is not obvious how we can or should include them when we think about cities. Therefore, we sought experts in these subjects. The study of social equity was prepared by Alan Ryan, a political philosopher at the Princeton University Center for Human Values, and the paper on environmental health was prepared by John Spengler and Tim Ford, environmental scientists at the Harvard School of Public Health.

The growth and form of North American cities are analyzed in five case studies: New York, Toronto, Cascadia, Mexico City, and Los Angeles. They interweave the physical and social, the built and the natural environment. They raise questions about economic and sustainable development, civil society and governance. The contrasts among the five cities are striking. But they have a common characteristic—they are all now city-regions.

Twenty years ago, for the Habitat I conference in Vancouver, Barbara Ward wrote in *The Home of Man* that "mankind is engaged in a kind of race for survival, between the inner and outer boundaries of *social* pressures and *physical* constraints, while the doubling of population and the emergence of a half-urban world takes place. These overlapping contexts of violent demographic, social, and environmental change all meet—one could say collide—in human settlements."

Today, we are facing two critical issues of urban growth and form—on the one hand, extreme concentrations, and on the other hand, extreme separations. The concentrations—of people, cars, and settlements—result in environmental pollution and ecological risk. The separations—of economic classes, racial and ethnic minorities—result in social inequity, isolation, and loss of community.

The case studies illuminate the dilemma of having both concentrations and separations. For example, one case study describes an urban form organized according to economic class, with the upper class moving away from the public realm, toward privatization expressed by closed urban areas and controlled access gates. Lester Thurow believes that there are now 30,000 walled-off communities in the United States. Another case study cites "the ever-widening social chasm" of millions of people living economically below the poverty line, socially in dysfunctional districts, spatially separated from jobs, education, recreation, and the benefits of city-life. These separations are described, in another case study, as "racism and violence in American culture expressed in spatial terms."

In several cases a new paradigm for city-regions is emerging. Its goal is the balance of three factors: economy, environment, and equity. The balance has not yet been achieved. Urban development since World War II has been dominated by only one of the three factors, economy.

The environmental movement in recent years has sought to redress the balance. There is widespread agreement on goals, but not yet on the means of achieving equilibrium. What should be the growth and form of an *ecological* city-region?

Now, a third factor—social equity—introduces new issues. Economy and environment, yes, but for whom? What should be the growth and form of a *fair, just, democratic* city-region?

The city today is a product of the 19th century's industrial revolution, which centralized the activities of production and exchange, and the 20th century's technological revolutions in transportation and communication, which decentralized these activities. This urban implosion and explosion is unlike anything in the past, when cities and towns were relatively static in their form, and their growth was in predictably concentric rings. Now, the dynamic growth of human settlements knows no bounds; because its *form* is in doubt, it raises fundamental questions about the *city-region*.

Social equity? If, as social scientists predict, the future organization of work will be more akin to preindustrial cities (having an intimate mix rather than separation of places for home and work), then open access to many types of *centers* will be necessary for a democratic society. More than ever we will need places to meet, to exchange, to see and hear each other, to *be* together.

Environmental health? If, as scientists predict, the unprecedented explosion of human settlements threatens our natural and built habitat, limits and *edges* of many types—the urban growth boundary, the forest edge, the shore-line—will be necessary for our survival.

Taken together, *centers* and *edges* can be the best—the most fair and healthy—prescription for the future of city-regions.

ROBERT GEDDES

Acknowledgments

The Conference on Cities in North America (CCNA) originated in discussions between the United Nations Centre for Human Settlements and an inter-university consortium of the following faculty from Harvard University; the University of California, Berkeley; Columbia University; and New York University: Thomas Bender (New York University), Kenneth Frampton (Columbia University), Robert Geddes (New York Institute for the Humanities at NYU), Donlyn Lyndon (University of California, Berkeley), Peter Rowe (Harvard University), Aliye Pekin Celik (United Nations Centre for Human Settlements, New York).

The New York Institute for the Humanities at NYU sponsored the CCNA and the publication of its *Working Papers*. In particular, our gratitude is extended to the following: Tony Judt, Director; Anne Hollander, Acting Director; Jocelyn Carlson Baltzell, Associate Director; and staff members Kate Houghton and Sarah Sweeny.

Support for the CCNA came from the New York Institute for the Humanities at NYU; the John D. and Catherine T. MacArthur Foundation; the Daniel and Joanna Rose Fund; Harvard University, Graduate School of Design; and New York University, Faculty of Arts and Science.

ROBERT GEDDES
DIRECTOR, CCNA

Introduction

Ellen Posner

=====

North American cities have a special place in the world's imagination. They may not be the most glorious repositories of culture or history, but they do stand out in a spectacular way as displays of artifice, technology, and marshaling of resources. Especially in the abstraction of darkness, and with the assistance of artificial illumination, New York and Los Angeles, for example, shimmer with evidence of American economic power in the 20th century.

Manhattan's lineup of exotic corporate towers, punctuating the delicate web of nighttime lights embedded in its slender man-made canyons; LA's blanket of lights, spread over an improbable swath of desert, from the mountains to the sea—these are images of our era and they are recognizable anywhere. The world's financial capital on one coast, its capital of entertainment and fantasy on the other. Even longtime residents of either city are susceptible to jolts of excitement as these cities come into view.

At the edge of the 21st century, though, there are conditions that, if sufficiently known and understood, can make either one of those images seem to be a mirage. The cities of North America—even its most famous and vaunted cities—are being affected by the same powerful economic, political, and social forces that are transforming cities all over the world. Global economic restructuring, the changing nature of capitalism, the impact of technology, the migration of people across borders: these are some of the phenomena that are beginning to give shape to the urban landscape of the next millennium.

These phenomena, however, tend to be at once intriguingly complex and still in the process of unfolding. For instance, global economic restructuring, which is often used as a vague catchall term, refers to a variety of changing circumstances, some of which can be discerned, some not. So far, though, it does seem that the increasingly global nature of the world economy—with its emphasis on free trade, elimination of protectionist barriers, increased

1

mobility of private capital, dominance of transnational corporations and transactions involving finance rather than manufacturing—is giving cities, including the cities of North America, heightened roles to play.

Cities have become increasingly important as centers of control for a wide range of financial transactions, as headquarters for clusters of financial and related businesses and for businesses that generate media and technology. Cities must therefore cope with a high concentration of specialized activities and accommodation of the population that they require. Some strengths are then exaggerated, but also vulnerabilities. The power of physical proximity, of the range of dynamic encounters that are unique to an urban environment, is underscored, but it is also easy to see the effects on a city's physical fabric when particular economic interests prevail.

A 1996 United Nations report notes that while cities that can compete successfully for international and national investment will have great advantages, the current emphasis on free markets also results in "governments with less power and private capital with greater power." That power shift can affect what is funded, what is built. According to Saskia Sassen, in *The Global City*, it has already resulted in "a new spatial unevenness," with the development of "large-scale, high-cost luxury office and residential complexes" at the same time that other parts of cities, not adjacent to those complexes, descend into physical decay.

The surge in migration, the flow of people across national borders and within individual countries everywhere, for myriad reasons, also is having a profound impact on the cities of North America—especially, but not exclusively, on gateway cities such as New York, Los Angeles, Toronto, and Vancouver. And, like global economic restructuring, migration is a complex phenomenon.

Migration has been spurred by the end of colonialism and of the Cold War, but also by wars and political upheaval and by various kinds of social change, including the rate at which households break up and the number of times that people now change jobs. Migrants may be refugees, asylum seekers, students, skilled professionals who can go wherever the best opportunities present themselves, or people seeking to rejoin their families or to find a better life. Some of the changes are so new that accurate calculation and description is very challenging. So much is happening at once that old ways of understanding no longer seem useful.

As never before, inhabitants of cities of every size are, more and more, faced with the presence of those who are ethnically and economically different from themselves. Increased cultural and even economic vibrancy are likely to emerge from increasing migration—but so is the potential for social tension and social fragmentation.

In North America, as elsewhere, one of the essential variables in this discussion is how "city" or "urban center" is defined. The idea of a core city and its surrounding suburbs and towns constituting a single metropolitan region has certainly been gaining acceptance. There is a growing understanding of how much is shared: infrastructure, the consequences of environmental dilemmas, opportunities for employment and, therefore, overall economic status, and (albeit at the periphery of awareness) the danger resulting from continuing social fragmentation. And yet United Nations research, while addressing urbanization and the growth of cities, suggests caution in assuming that soon more people will be living in cities than in rural areas. The numbers depend upon what actually constitutes an urban center and what the boundaries of that physical entity are assumed to be. If a densely populated country such as China or India were to change its own definitions, global statistics would instantly be altered. Estimating the size or population of a city depends on where you place the boundaries, what you include. The lines are not drawn firmly; the actual size of any single metropolitan area is open to interpretation. Therefore, so is its population.

These vast metropolitan regions also present a great challenge to the planner. Since most cities are not governed by any single metropolitan entity, there is, inevitably, fragmentation, overlap, and questions about who exactly is in charge. The size and scale of these regions, the competing interests and complexity of needs tend to make old ideas about cities seem irrelevant. Flexibility, the capacity to respond to rapid change, and a willingness to establish and work with a vision of the future, rather than a blueprint for it, are most likely to be assets in addressing an unwieldy urban situation.

Among the many incongruities of the late 20th century, however, is the co-existence of efforts to understand and to intervene in—and even to shape— the great collective undertakings that are cities, and what appears to be our steadily decreasing ability to see ourselves as a society.

Saskia Sassen's description of "a new spatial unevenness" in the city itself can seem almost mild in relation to what is occurring in surrounding areas: gated communities in Los Angeles; what Ethan Seltzer (see the Cascadia case study) describes as the establishment of "economic monocultures" outside Portland; and the move of affluent citizens to farther and farther edges of metropolitan areas accompanied by the businesses and services that follow them, which Jonathan Barnett (see the New York case study) has described as not merely the making of a suburb but actually the making of "a parallel universe."

The future is unknown. But there are already many surprises. When the United Nations convened its first summit on cities in 1976, the prevailing belief was that the cities of Europe and North America had much to teach the developing world—that these cities served as examples of how to build, live in, and manage cities, which others should follow. Those in the cities of developing countries looked then and still look now to the cities of the North. They can hardly escape. The images are ubiquitous and indelible. But while 20 years ago the expectation was that they would learn from us, that urban environments everywhere would be lifted to (or near) exalted heights of the famous powerhouses by the end of the 20th century, what actually has happened is that there has been leveling downward. Following the Conference on Cites in North America (CCNA), Kenneth Greenberg (see the Toronto case study) observed that what the cities of North America ought really to bring to a global discussion is "a critical reflection on what is happening to us, rather than a discussion of our accomplishments." Jonathan Barnett (see the New York case study) pointed out that North American cities can serve as "a warning" of how "you can have these resources—and squander them."

Twenty years ago, as awareness increased and hopefulness surged, it would have been thought unlikely that at the end of the 20th century North American cities would be facing serious problems of pollution and environmental degradation, including threatened water supplies, and would in many cases lack the consensus or the will to clean up the mess.

We did not expect to see an antique infrastructure patched together on an as-needed, crisis-by-crisis basis—exploding water pipes, crashing trains, or, since the problems were noticed and appeared to have remedies, widespread poverty (the National Coalition for the Homeless estimates that there are 3 million homeless in the United States and 250,000 in Canada, where the Scandinavian model safety net has begun to fray). Nor was it obvious that a changing economy would bring back sweatshops and even conditions that can only be described as slavery—very often in locations not far from dazzling corporate towers and elaborate art museums—or that we would arrive at this moment and find that one of the most significant factors shaping the configuration not only of cities but of entire regions is the determination of "haves" to separate themselves from "have-nots."

As a result, when we look ahead now and discuss what a city can be or ought to be in the 21st century, who and what it must accommodate, and how, what its role is nationally and globally, we are led back to some of the most fundamental human questions: how we choose to live and what we value.

A discussion of North American cities has been long overdue. In the United States, particularly, because of a deep suspicion of the metropolis, which may be rooted in an early idea of America as Arcadia, or in a strong belief in individualism, there has been a longstanding policy of having no urban policy. And so, in the course of the last decade, even as the stakes have risen, American architects and planners have been left to simply watch in frustration as cities in Europe and Asia plan aggressively for the 21st century.

It isn't as though our counterparts elsewhere actually know any more than we about what to expect or what ought to be done. But they have at least been making their best guess and acting on some prevailing assumptions: that, as national boundaries blur, the world will be connected by a network of cities, and that in order to be ascendant or included in that high-power global network, there are a number of things a city must do. It must establish a contemporary urban identity, become or remain known as a place where talented people want to be, and demonstrate an ability to attract its share of global capital.

Marketing and imagery have become highly valued by cities seeking to find a place for themselves in the landscape of the 21st century: visual elements, especially architectural elements, that lend themselves to multiple reproduction in various media are in demand. Up-to-date infrastructure; transportation that works; and even education, health care, and a significant cultural life are factors that can be helpful.

The extent to which the basics are important should not be underestimated. Research done by the United Nations, for instance, resulted in a warning to cities not to put excessive emphasis on technology in their race to be competitive—since technology is quickly outdated, and future requirements are truly unpredictable. As Robert Yaro (see the New York case study) observed during a meeting that followed CCNA, "Nobody knows what is coming next in terms of technology, communications, etc." Attempting to plan for those variables, he said, "means getting into realms of abstraction as we get farther and farther away from what we know."

Clean streets, inviting public spaces (including parks and beaches), the cultivation of an array of shops and restaurants are still considered to be the sort of amenities that cities should be able to offer. They are the basic components of civilized urban life. Some significant American cities, including New York, have a long way to go if they are going to catch up in these areas, as well as in infrastructure.

The competition already is fierce. And North American architects and planners who recognize the importance of cities and who know that North American cities are not merely going to be in a race with each other but are going to have to compete with London, Frankfurt, Singapore, Rotterdam, and Tokyo understand that complacency is a dangerous course.

As ideas about what cities are, or ought to be, evolve, traditional planning strategies seem less and less appropriate. As our cities struggle to cast themselves forward into a mysterious future, it would seem reasonable to expect to see some interesting experimentation. There is a shortage of brilliant ideas, though, or at least support for them. And the tendency is instead toward a prevailing sameness.

The requisite waterfront development, the aquarium, food halls, festival marketplace, convention center, overblown office and residential complex with hotel—they are everywhere. They are geared, to a high degree, toward bolstering tourism, which means that they may not be especially meaningful or engaging to those who live in a particular city. Cities show their links to each other by exhibiting branches of the same shops and the same restaurants and buildings designed by the same architects. And those repetitive, unimaginative approaches suggest a widespread reluctance to confront serious issues—issues that are not going to go away. The disconcerting emphasis on entertainment, on the commercially acceptable, the meretricious, at the expense of dealing with the nature of public space, the effect of urban systems on the environment, the provision of adequate housing, leads to a vague sense of unease about who exactly is in charge and whether anyone is paying attention.

Questions about how much control can be exercised over the configuration of a large dense city and its greater metropolitan area have new urgency. Richard Weinstein (see the Los Angeles case study) suggests that "a kind of uncertainty principle should affect the attitude of urban designers and planners as they approach the problem of the extended city," and that they should prepare themselves to face up to urban spaces that "aren't perfect, that are messy, contingent, that live for ten years and then disappear." Gardner Church (see the Toronto case study) observes that "Governing an urban region is about managing surprising events *after* the best efforts at holistic planning."

And a fierce debate arose at CCNA over how a city's leftover, abandoned, interstitial, inexpensive spaces should be regarded. Whether those odd bits and partially run-down spaces ought to be recognized as a means of accommodating entrepreneurship and the increasing contingent and flexible elements of the contemporary economy and therefore as candidates for limited or no intervention; or whether they should be targeted for improvement and investment.

Los Angeles, because of a climate that allows for the use of inexpensive materials and an extended framework that accepts disorder, has its own brand of run-down and leftover spaces. Many were nothing much to begin with. New York's leftover spaces are more likely to have been structures or neighborhoods of some substance. There is the concern, in those cases, that nonintervention would mean, as Jonathan Barnett said, abandoning once-valued spaces "to the cruelties of the real estate market."

But the cruelties of the real estate market may be in the eye of the beholder. As manufacturers moved out of the industrial buildings in New York's Soho district and as artists began, in a very informal way, to inhabit the large, bare, inexpensive spaces they had left behind, an interesting and vibrant new urban community established itself, and small businesses that could serve that community followed. Soho's subsequent appeal to a more affluent population, its sprucing up, its rising real estate value, and the appearance of pricey shops and representatives of chain stores have made it far less intriguing.

The gritty but authentic South Street Seaport, not far from Soho, was a compelling urban edge, a place for exploring, a home to quirky commercial enterprises—until it was eviscerated by a festival marketplace, fast-food restaurants, and other tourist attractions.

And Times Square—an idea almost as much as a place—was one of New York's great draws. Its first-run movies, restaurants, and proximity to the theater district, mixed in with X-rated adult entertainment and seedy bars and its once-famous neon signs, gave it a racy rather than scary quality. It also became a place in which artists could find studio space after Soho became too expensive. As legitimate businesses, including restaurants, were closed down in preparation for an upscale surge, streets were left blank and truly unwelcoming. Slowly, buildings renovated to pristine showiness and shops and attractions decorated in innocent pastel colors and meant for tourists are contributing to a flattening out, lifelessness, lack of authenticity. Without making a case for dereliction, it can be argued that the unique drama of urban life is supported by surprises, by uneasy transitions, by some raw spaces with open-ended futures.

With very little consensus, though, about how to proceed, even in the heart of the city itself, it is not at all surprising that discussions about strategies for the outer rings, the smaller towns and communities that constitute a great metropolitan area, seem even more tentative.

Efforts at regional planning confront the conflict between enlightened collective interest and the demands of the marketplace, between control of the landscape and the widespread appeal of the single-family home, the impulse to create and flee to economic monocultures, the choices made by businesses.

Paying attention to cities has never been more important. Whether the extent of urbanism in our time is due to mobility, fertility, the stretching of boundaries or of definitions, a vast number of people now live and work in urban areas—and cities continue to grow in economic, political, and social importance.

These variables are dynamic in North America, which has some of the fastest growing cities and metropolitan areas in the world. Seattle, Miami, Phoenix, Los Angeles, Houston, and Atlanta, for instance, did not exist or . were merely dots on the map in the last century. And, as research done by the United Nations stresses, "over the last few decades, both the United States and Canada experienced a much more rapid and fundamental reordering of their population and urban systems than Europe," with both countries having "cities in flux" as well as urban systems and metropolitan forms "still in the making."

All of this activity despite predictions that technology would make cities obsolete. As *The Economist's* 1995 survey on cities ("Turn up the Lights") explains, even though "money can fly around the world in nanoseconds," financial markets still demonstrate the importance of the city. "Many of the skills which matter in banking are personal. Someone who has spent a day in fruitless meetings might discover a vital nugget of information in a chance conversation by the coffee machine. Serendipitous proximity cannot be reproduced by fax machine or video-conferencing." The concept of "urbanity" is still considered desirable: vibrancy, action, heterogeneity, sophistication, interesting things happening everywhere. As Jonathan Barnett stressed at CCNA, "Cities are not just good, but essential" in that they represent "committed resources that we already have."

That view really is at the heart of the matter. As Lewis Mumford pointed out years ago in *The City in History,* at the time that capitalism first began to emerge, when land became a mere commodity rather than a stewardship, and when transactions became anonymous, the new entrepreneurs very much "needed the old cities." The profits were there, the consumers were there, the structures that already existed represented huge capital investments.

More recently, Saskia Sassen has noted in *The Global City* that one element of our current global economic restructuring, "the massive increase in the volume of transactions in the financial industry" that has followed widespread deregulation, has made cities more rather than less important. Cities are needed as the central places in which those transactions are overseen and controlled and also as the places where all of the ancillary "producer services" necessary to the financial industry can cluster. Sassen also explains, though, that "Almost half the jobs in the producer services are lower income jobs," that a "vast supply of low-wage jobs are required by high-income gentrification in both its residential and commercial settings." Whereas manufacturing generated "a large number of middle class jobs."

Such observations remind us how important it is at the end of the 20th century to recognize that aesthetic and formal concerns cannot be separated from social, economic, and environmental concerns, or from issues of equity. Part of the agenda for CCNA was to try to understand the ways in which those issues are intertwined with the fate of cities and regions.

There is an element of sadness in the realization that, even now, a consideration of "social equity" and of "justice" can be treated almost as if it is a new idea—notwithstanding the teachings of ancient religious traditions.

Architects confronted with discussions of social equity find themselves in an awkward—but not uninteresting—position. As members of a profession that is currently without an ethic, they have not been driving the discussion. Commissioned by clients to install barrier walls and private pathways that can keep out or discourage those who are unwanted or hired to create private commercial experiences out of what might have been public space, many become complicit in structuring the urban language of separation.

As conversation proceeds, though, there is occasion for architects to question their roles, to think about what interventions they can make in the urban fabric, what ideas they can contribute. Either do so or be left to decorate the edges of a brutal world.

The time is right for self-examination within other disciplines as well. At CCNA, John Spengler said that, looking at the serious problems of environmental degradation that we now face, he didn't think the institutional structure that we rely on—the United Nations, the World Health Organization, universities around the United States—were "young, vital, healthy enough" to make a difference. And with, as he observed, a citizenry that is largely resistant to change, limited commitment of either the private or public sector, the prevalence of short-term thinking, not to mention the emergence of new drug-resistant pathogens and the globalization that brings them ever closer, there is an urgent need for clear strong voices, of the kind of informed participation that not only isolates the mechanisms for change, but that can also work to encourage the ideology that creates a determination for change.

And even more alarming than photographs of a thick, nitrogen oxide haze over Washington, D.C., or dense smog locked in over Los Angeles is the knowledge that federal agencies now view environmental threats as, potentially, igniters of "hot" wars, just as military threats have been in the past. Conflicts over resources and living conditions, over arable land, clean water (or any water), and the various hazards associated with overcrowding are expected to be the sources of great clashes in coming decades, with cities and their regions at the very center, as focal points and targets.

There is serious speculation, and some alarming possibilities have been identified. But it is not at all clear where or how these conflicts will unfold. This makes the subject very challenging to discuss, much like other mysterious aspects of the urban situation as we near the 21st century.

Discussions about the dilemmas and potential dilemmas that face us all are made even more difficult, though, by the widening gulf between economic strata and by the predicted disappearance of a solid middle class. Issues of equity, of who a city is for, whose interests should be served, and the interconnected issue of how environmental concerns are dealt with seem less easily resolved, less obvious, less clear.

One of the central and most heated arguments at CCNA, for instance, was about the meaning of the phrase "quality of life." Piping in with exasperation after hearing the phrase used several times, Richard Weinstein said "Quality of life is a middle class notion." Most of the people in this world are poor, and their primary concern is to "put bread on the table," he said. "People will choose the right to work over the environment and quality of life as we define it every day of the week in most of the world."

An earlier report in *The Wall Street Journal* had supported that argument. Describing the multiple threats that Mexico City faces from smog, gridlock, and water shortages, with "blue skies a thing of the past," it pointed out that the city also was absorbing possibly the largest demographic explosion in history. Even with the knowledge of how polluted the air might be and what traffic nightmares they might have to face, people from elsewhere were still flooding into Mexico City in the hope of a better life for themselves and their children. Their hopes were being reinforced by the decisions businesses were making to stay in Mexico City primarily for the unique proximity (suppliers to retailers, for instance) that a city affords.

The tension that was created at CCNA, even between persons having similar economic and social positions, over what expectations we can have for the future if a vast number of city dwellers feel that they do not have the economic luxury of paying attention to the most serious urban problems, is an indication of how difficult it is going to be to build consensus and effect change in the urban landscape of the next century.

There are choices to be made about whether urban life will be shaped by a tacit acceptance of survival strategies—an underground economy, sweatshops, informal housing, urban agriculture, fixed-as-needed infrastructure, along with, of course, more surveillance cameras and armed guards—or by our collective aspirations. Even the first step, identifying what those aspirations actually are, will be challenging at a time when so many things appear to be in transition all at once.

Questions about what cities can and must do to fulfill those unidentified aspirations, to provide evidence of political and economic power, to serve as economic engines and as settings for democracy, to enable culture to flourish and discourse to take place, and to establish the underpinnings of a civilized life for all are on the table.

There is awareness, though, that cities will take center stage in coming decades—that they will be the places in which megatrends of the next century unfold, and that they will test our abilities to deal with life's most serious issues.

Since so many questions are unresolved, and since the stakes are so high, it is helpful to see disparate but important North American cities begin to recognize what strategies must be left behind, and begin to develop new strategies, new approaches, new ways of thinking about urban matters. The dialog offers evidence that these early steps forward, along with the realization of the place of the metropolis in the landscape of the 21st century, will lead to increasingly complex discussions, to informative struggles over physical form, over forms of governance, and over necessary policies on social equity and environmental health. Such struggles can loosen the hold that nostalgia has on us and open the way for an acceptance of new ideas and a determined effort to locate the source of political will.

Through the discussion of North American cities, begun here, we observe enormously important cities moving toward an uncertain future, asking the right questions.

Justice and the City

Alan Ryan

Every political theorist who takes an interest in classical political thinking starts with the thought that the city is the home of justice: that in the festivals and drama of the Athenians of the democratic era, it was presented as a place where *politics* is practiced and the patriarchal, vengeful, violent actions and reactions of warring families and their dependents have been brought under the rule of law. In the last pages of *Eumenides,* Athena comes to live in the city and tells the subjects of Theseus, the future Athenians, not only that they will become the "school of Hellas" that Pericles boasted of in his Funeral Oration, but that they will henceforth live under the rule of justice. They will exchange good for good, each contributing to the common weal and sharing in it. A just order will replace the rule of passion and the law will replace vengeance.

Although *Eumenides* is my favorite dramatic text for obvious reasons, this theme reverberates in other plays. In our century conscientious disobedience has become one of the ways in which citizens can protest bad law and dissociate themselves from tyranny; so the person and character of Antigone is especially engrossing to us. A cooler, perhaps more historical reading of Antigone might suggest that its most sharply political implication was the need to get out of a world in which family ties and political authority were too tightly linked; the tyranny and pride that stemmed from familial politics would breed endless cycles of death and resistance and rebellion. If life were to go on, only lawful rule was tolerable. Antigone was both a heroine and a fatally self-destructive character; in a lawful state, family strife would not threaten the fabric of the polity and would not provoke the kind of moral disaster that the play depicts.

It did not and does not follow that only *democratic* politics are tolerable. The Greeks recognized that constitutional politics might be of almost any

kind, so long as they subordinated ambition to the rule of law and preserved
a sharp distinction between the wishes *de facto* of the ruling elite and the laws
de jure that governed society. One consequence of the creation of the *polis* was
the growth of political discussion and thus of arguments within political theory about the justice of different political arrangements: aristocratic, monarchical, democratic. Since what follows is concerned almost exclusively with
theories of *distributive* or *economic* justice, I ought to say now that this is not
to slight theories of political justice but merely to clear enough space to deal
with the subject at hand. My thought is that the technological and economic
changes of the past 30 to 50 years, no doubt in conjunction with cultural
shifts of various kinds, have posed distinctive problems for *urban* and *regional*
planners and thinkers, and that these changes characteristically raise questions in distributive justice. The same considerations do not apply—at any
rate not directly—to the justice of political arrangements. If representative
democracy is uniquely just, then it will be just for the government of the city
and region as well as that of the county, the state, and the whole country; my
focus is on the problems of equity posed by the modern city and region.

There is one feature of classical Greek views of democratic, aristocratic,
and monarchical forms of justice that I shall want to borrow later. All these
conceptions of political justice have implications for the shape and function-
ing of the city. The Spartans were proud of the fact that they had no city
walls: "every man a brick." The absent walls were a visible symbol of the
Spartan conviction that every citizen would die before he or she abandoned
the post assigned to him or her. It was not only absent walls that were a pow-
erfully present symbol. The Athenians' Long Walls that connected Athens
and the Piraeus, which were built after the Persians had taken the city during the Persian Wars, were a military necessity, and they certainly would not
have been built unless the Athenians had required a protected route to their
ships. Once built, they symbolized the Athenians' energy and ingenuity and
were a source of civic pride as well as of simple protection.

Similarly, the Acropolis was more than an expression of Athenian power
and more than "just" a site for assorted ritual observances. It was the city's
image of itself made concrete. Critics of Athenian imperialism, from the
Melians to Lewis Mumford, have always said, and rightly so, that part of what
the Acropolis made concrete was Athenian *hubris,* that it was an unabashed,
self-congratulatory display of Athens's domination of her notional allies, and
a standing invitation to divine retribution. It was also a visible expression of
the idea that the city would live under law, following a system of rules that
made even the government of one man or a few men a lawful form of rule

and one that operates in the interests of all. The specifically democratic quality of Athenian politics shone a vivid light on the fact that the *agora* was the physical hub of decision-making; the mixture of everyday commercial activity and political activity was one example of bringing decision-making into the street and giving it to the common man. The implications of these facts for ways in which *we* might think about *democratic* justice are far from clear to me, but they are certainly thought provoking.

Justice Made Visible

Political theorists have generally been interested in moral hierarchy rather than in city planning; but there are many examples of their taking it for granted that a society's moral commitments will be visibly expressed in its technology and in its domestic and public accommodations. One engaging and recurring trope in utopian thought is the suggestion that a serious society will make its chamber pots of gold. Plato's *Republic* complained about Athenian urban congestion as part of his more general denunciation of a changeable commercial society. Plato maintained that the bustle was all part of a general contempt for a proper hierarchy, a hierarchy so violated that donkeys pushed pedestrians off the sidewalks. It was a common conservative complaint that in Athens it had become impossible to distinguish between slaves and free men, and Plato was having fun embroidering that complaint.

We should immediately acknowledge an obvious dichotomy between the normative and the diagnostic. We should distinguish two different thoughts: the first, that the city *should* display a physical order that will reflect the commitments of, and have a moral effect on, the inhabitants of the area; the second, that we can as a matter of fact read the commitments of a given society in its city planning. A humdrum instance would contrast the view from the train window on the journey between Princeton and New York with what can be seen in the outskirts of Berne or Basel. Miles of urban dereliction, abandoned factories, and insanitary-looking housing would suggest to almost any observer either that the population revels in making a mess of the environment and then abandoning it to go and make another mess elsewhere, or else that the political and economic system is so contrived that it ignores wishes of its citizens for more attractive rather than less attractive surroundings or to live tidily and elegantly rather than in a chaotic mess.

On a less humdrum level, Renaissance writers and painters in the utopian mould appeared to think that a radial plan, or a clearly marked grid, expresses the rationality of the city, and lends rationality to the city in turn; in an appropriate streetscape, the eye would be led—as it is led by the light of the sun—to consider the seat of authority and fount of wisdom at the heart of the city, or led toward the port through which the city's commerce flows, or out into the countryside that the city protects and governs. In their survey of utopian theorists from the ancient world to the present, the Manuels dwell on the theorists of the *città felice*, architectural thinkers who believed that the built environment of the ideal city would indeed reflect and instill in the citizens the moral commitments on whose basis the city was built. One can see the point made in reverse in William Morris's *News from Nowhere*, described by may critics as a "pastoral version of Marx's *Capital*." Cities are visible only in the distance, and a stroll along the Thames ends at a harvest supper in Morris's home, Kelmscott. In Morris's utopia, there is need of neither law nor justice nor the state; we revert to a rural and pre-Athenian past, but without the half-mad heroes and pirates from whom the *polis* rescued us.

Among modern writers, one whose visual (and narrative) imagination was of the slightest, but one who laid out his utopia with enough local color to drive Morris to rebuttal was Edward Bellamy. His immensely successful utopian fantasy was published in 1888; *Looking Backward* described Boston in the year 2000 as it had become after the triumph of the corporate socialism that Bellamy called "nationalism." (Bellamy knew that what he was describing was socialism, but thought that the term "socialism" conjured up images of beards and free love, and that his readers would be happier with "nationalism"; since the book was second only to *Uncle Tom's Cabin* among American best-sellers in the 19th century, and sold 200,000 copies in the first two years, one can't really complain.) In the absence of descriptive detail in *Looking Backward*'s accounts of visits to shops and eating places, it is impossible to say exactly what sort of architecture Bellamy had in mind for the year 2000. The suspicion that it was some form of debased neo-classicism makes it hard to read *Looking Backward* without seeing its architecture through the lenses of Reagan-era Washington. Still, this is unfair, since Bellamy's nationalism was not the cowboy imperialism of Reagan, and even if Bellamy hankered after the classical, the current craze for post-modern classical pastiche commercial architecture had not reared its irritating head in the 1880s.

Bellamy's nationalism was the view that an ethos of public service, and the disciplined corporate organization of late 19th century capitalism, pressed to its limit, were the only possible basis for an industrial society, and Bellamy's vision of revitalized Boston was of a city that expressed these values. Soldiers and workers must share the same spirit; managers and generals were as one. Presidents of the Republic and presidents of General Motors were the bearers of the same organizational ethos. It was to be a world of bureaucratic, scientific, meritocratic rationalism, and the architectural and country-wide planning system lightly sketched in *Looking Backward* reflected those virtues.

The prevailing atmosphere, both in Bellamy's social theory and in his sketch of the new Boston, is an obsession with uniformity, regularity, and hygiene; this is emphasized by the burial of utilities, and a kind of "factory in a garden" form of planned landscape that spreads as far as the eye can see. It is the visible embodiment of one sort of justice—the justice expressed in strict economic equality. It is a moot point whether Bellamy abolished wage labor in his utopia; on the one hand, he was concerned to abolish *money,* but on the other, he had none of Marx's hatred of exchanging labor for the means of life. What is not moot is that Bellamy tried to square the circle by appealing both to American individualism and the new corporatist enthusiasm: each worker could choose just what occupation to take up as long as it lay within his abilities, but the "income" the worker got was exactly the same as everyone else's. Hours were adjusted to bring supply and demand into balance; the great anti-capitalist and anti-entrepreneurial assumption was that public demand for goods and services was predictable enough to enable the planners to know in advance how much labor was needed.

Everything in *Looking Backward* was organized in such a way as to emphasize the individual's dependence on public provision, even though—as witnessed by Bellamy's account of shopping and dining in utopia, and his chilling account of the way piped music was to replace the concert hall—everyday consumption was more privatized than under capitalism. The basic rule is that each person is entitled to exactly the same share of the public cake as everyone else; since this is a utopia for Americans, the form this takes is that everyone received a credit card loaded with the same value as everyone else's.

Interestingly, Bellamy's utopia showed another form of imaginative decay that one might complain of in the architecture of Washington, D.C. Actual European cities ordinarily contained a central square wherein the people might assemble, or to which they might be summoned by their oligarchical rulers, in order to witness the exemplary punishment of traitors or hear the news of some triumph or disaster or whatever else their public life involved. These are spaces on a scale that suggests that 10,000 to 20,000 people would be at the upper bound of a possible assembly, and a much lower figure would feel like a decent crowd. In many medieval Italian cities, much as in ancient Athens, squares did double duty as marketplace and arena for politics. Elsewhere, the politics might be in part divine politics, as in the case of the Pope's appearances on the balcony of St. Peter's, and the life and death appearances of Savonarola.

In Washington there is no such space. Nor has there been in London following the rebuilding of Parliament after the fire of 1836. Speaker's Corner in Hyde Park is a refuge for the eccentric, and Trafalgar Square is the only central focus for demonstrations of popular disaffection. The VE celebrations in May 1945 took place in Whitehall and required impromptu arrangements for Churchill's appearance. The royal family, on the other hand, frequently appeared on the balcony of Buckingham Palace, where the public was never within a hundred yards of them; the traffic island by the Victoria Monument is not a political space.

The Washington Mall is an excellent place for demonstrations, or was so in 1963 and 1967, as was the Pentagon lawn; but it is not a place for rulers and ruled to communicate with each other. The whole Capitol area is evidently a schizophrenic construction, being an imperial monument to a folksy ideal of democracy. It seems quite proper that it has no forum to front onto, seeing that the people for whom the legislators are to deliberate are anything up to two and a half thousand miles and more away.

Perhaps we ought not be shocked by this. I am no enthusiast for the plebiscitary direct democracy that Castro used to practice in late 1960s Havana and that Roberto Michels advocated in the 1920s. We have long left the world of the city-state. Sheer numbers make it silly to regret this fact. Still, we might wonder why we are so addicted to a form of civic architecture that is borrowed at third hand—a Frenchman's overblown neo-classicism. It is the architecture of *imperial* Rome, a style apt enough for an absolutist state where a passive mass is asked to stare at and be overwhelmed by the buildings housing their rulers, perhaps apt enough for *ancien régime* or Napoleonic France and even on some construals for the Jacobin state, but hardly for a Jeffersonian democracy. *L'état, c'est nous* is in any case a difficult thought to construe. In Bellamy's utopia, and I think perhaps in Washington actuality, the best we can do is admire symbols of power, efficiency, competence, and order. Bellamy was light years away from believing in participatory democracy or indeed in democracy of any sort, so it is hardly a great deficiency that he has no democratic architectural vision. By the same token one might think that the architecture of Washington is no more morally suspect than that of imperial Athens.

John Rawls and Robert Nozick

I want to hang on to the distinction between normative theories of the way justice *ought* to be visible and empirical theories of the way it nevertheless *is* visible, while turning to a very brief account of recent theories of justice; the two questions I have in view are (1) what does a theory imply for the way we *ought* to structure the city?; and (2) what in a city's organization and appearance might lead us to believe that its inhabitants and/or their government subscribed to one or another theory? Needless to say, this second question is likely to lead one into flights of speculative fancy.

Nozick and Justice

I begin with Robert Nozick's account of justice, though I shall argue, perhaps perversely, and perhaps usefully, that it is interesting just because it has so few implications for the visibility of justice in the physical layout and economic activities of the city and region. Among dazzling intellectual performances, Robert Nozick's *Anarchy, State and Utopia* (1974) ranks very highly. It defends an individualist and near-anarchist vision of a just social order that challenges nearly every assumption held by planners and urbanists—or at least of those I grew up with in post-war Britain. It does so by founding everything on a version of the doctrine of the sanctity of property. It is thus a philosopher's extension in extreme form of ideas that are familiar to most people under the libertarian label.

Its basic intuition is that individuals are *self-owned*; we have a freehold in ourselves, and may do to and with ourselves whatever we choose as long as we don't violate other people's right to do the same kind of thing to themselves. The thought is that we can avoid problems of "competing" rights by explaining the rights we have in proprietary terms. Just as my ownership in my car doesn't extend to giving me a right to drive it over your lawn, and your right to your lawn doesn't extend to giving you a right to dig up my driveway and turf it over, so Nozick relies on the intuitive understanding of how one's property rights can be absolute without encroaching on anyone else's property rights, to give us absolute ownership of ourselves and therefore *not* of anyone else.

Nozick's understanding of ownership is modeled on orthodox old-fashioned English freeholds in fee simple. English property law is rather less clear than he suggests, but the basic intuitions serve his purposes well enough. In particular, they yield a "historical" theory of justice; *any* outcome (almost) can be just (i.e., almost any distribution of assets may be lawful). What matters is how it comes about. The basic claim is that if an initial distribution of rights did not violate justice, anything that results from legitimate exchanges is just. Suppose that a week ago you had a Cadillac and I had a bicycle; now the situation is reversed. This is unjust if I stole your car, but it is just if you gave it to me, or if you lost it in a (fairly conducted) wager with me, put it up as a prize which I won, and so on. Nozick asks us to see everything to which we have a right as part of our "holdings," an expression that reflects this proprietary conception of rights. The justice of any particular distribution of "holdings" is thus a matter of history. Since we own ourselves, our efforts and skills, and thus own the things we acquire by using them, understanding the justice of a situation is a matter of understanding the route by which we moved from an earlier set of "holdings" to a later set.

For our purposes, this has some interesting implications. The first of them is that we cannot read the justice of a city's arrangements by seeing who lives where and gets what. A discussion paper on regional equity produced by the Regional Plan Association takes it for granted that the tri-state (New York–New Jersey–Connecticut) urban region's resources are "inequitably" distributed. It lists a large number of distressing facts about the poverty and under-employment of the region and the hazards facing its children. It is impossible to deny that they attest to the existence of a great deal of misery and hard to believe that they represent a state of affairs that is other than "sub-optimal": the resources in the area could be used to make more people happier or better off. A believer in Nozickian theory of justice could readily assent to all that and still insist that this was not (at least by itself and without further argument) evidence that there was injustice or inequity in this distribution. For injustice to exist, "holdings" would have to be in "the wrong hands," and the criteria of "wrongness" would be quite narrow—people would have what was really someone else's and would have got it by force or fraud.

Consider a city in which the inhabitants subscribe to something like this conception of justice: justice as the unfettered use of wholly owned resources. In the process of using our resources as we choose, we are exposed to all the vagaries of good and bad luck, and what happens to the resources thus used will largely be unpredictable. Of 30 rock groups whose living conditions we examine today, 28 will be living in worse conditions five years later, one will be living in somewhat better conditions, and one will be living in some splendor; only if the successful group has bribed disc jockeys, sabotaged its competitors' road shows, or something of the sort can we properly say that its success represents an injustice to the others. This is not to say that the victors *deserve* their success. It may *only* be luck that has seen them home, and it is sure to be quite largely luck. To be lucky, however, is not to profit from injustice, and to be unlucky is not to be the victim of injustice. Thus, the mere existence of slums and mansions, vast tracts of decent middle-class housing or their absence, tell one nothing about the justice of the economic life of that city or region. (They may lead one to make conjectures, as we shall see; but the fact that, as Nozick says, his theory of justice is "non-patterned" and "historical" means that a city that subscribed to such a view would need to be understood historically rather than by reference to a synchronic pattern.) My suspicion is that Los Angeles would be the best case for Nozickian justice. The city and region could plausibly be represented as the accidental outcome of a relatively unconstrained use of their resources by persons who happened to settle there and go about their business as they chose.

This may suggest to the reader that planning is in principle anti-Nozickian. Many current writers are trying to hide behind the Fifth and Fourteenth Amendments in order to cripple environmental and other planning regulations in the name of the rule against "takings"; so, in a Nozickian world any use of property that is not consented to is an unlawful taking. Since the theory starts from the assumption that ownership, like self-possession, is unlimited in scope and consists of an arbitrary sovereignty limited only by the same right in others, it must view all regulations as a form of taking. If that is a cogent view, no planned city is consistent with Nozickian justice.

I think this is broadly right; it is certainly right in the context of *actual* zoning and planning regulations, where an owner may well find that he can no longer do with his property what he could have done when he bought it. Still, it is not strictly true as a matter of theory. Since history is everything here, we may imagine many routes by which planning can legitimately come into existence: that somebody or some group buys out the rights the planners require; or that the land on which the city stands is acquired by a freeholder who grants leases only on terms that the planning authority agrees to. Essentially, the thought is that a planning authority must get that authority from the voluntary acceptance of those over whom it is exercised, and that for it to run with the property, there must be some historical moment at which the owners of the property put it under that authority. Thereafter, whoever takes property by purchase takes it together with the restrictions that have been attached to it.

Hayek and Nozick's emphasis on the fact that it is largely *luck* that dictates winners and losers in a free market is intellectually sound but ideologically risky. It is clear enough that the difference between successful and unsuccessful entrepreneurs is largely luck—intelligent effort makes a difference, but any true entrepreneur is essentially a gambler who is betting his investment funds on an untested hypothesis about the public's tastes for new products. Wage earners are unconsenting gamblers, for they have no choice but to bet their futures on the success of their employers. But few non-theorists are entirely comfortable with the thought that the economy rests on the moral principles of the casino. The winners in the economic lottery do not believe that they are just lucky; like most people, they wish to see their success as something they deserve. Conversely, most people wish to believe that the unsuccessful have got their just deserts as well; and all current evidence is that the electorate tries to believe it no matter what intellectual contortions that requires. Eliza Doolittle's dustman father in *Pygmalion* was unusual in standing up for the rights of the undeserving poor (or if not for their *rights* at any rate for *them*).

The argument ought not to be exaggerated; in general, there will be some correlation between the things that we count as constituting deserts and success—hard work, good organization, persistence, forethought. Nonetheless, it will not be a very close correlation. The upshot of a stress on luck is not that *justice* demands the provision of a safety net but that *political prudence* requires such a provision, lest the disadvantaged turn against the system. F.A. von Hayek was, contrary to the belief of many of his admirers, a defender of the welfare state; but Hayek's argument for the welfare state was carefully distanced from any suggestion that is rested on "social justice." There was, he claimed, no such thing as social justice; creating a welfare state is a prudent response to the tensions that a regime of pure justice would create. One might imagine that a city built on pure Nozickian justice would not have a welfare department, while one built on Hayekian justice-cum-prudence would, but I leave these speculations to one side.

Rawlsian Justice

If Nozick's *Anarchy, State and Utopia* is the most dazzling account of justice in recent years, the most influential is John Rawls's. It has appeared in several versions, and its most recent version has withdrawn some of the seemingly radical economic implications of the first version—*Theory of Justice* (1971). The first version stressed what has become known as the "maximin" theory of justice: the thought that the economic order should be set up in such a way that the inequalities stemming from the cooperative employment of our distinctive talents should benefit the least advantaged to the greatest extent possible. The principle stresses that to the extent that we have some choice in the economic arrangements of our society, we should choose those that most benefit the least favored. Or, we should maximize the size of the minimum share of the economy's output. Since this is a *liberal* theory of justice, this distributive principle for economic affairs is subordinate to a more basic principle: that each person is entitled to the maximum liberty compatible with its equal distribution.

On some readings of what liberty involves, Rawls's insistence on the priority of liberty overwhelms the maximin theory of distribution; if each person were entitled to employ his or her resources as he or she chose, there would be nothing for the maximin principle to apply to and Rawls's theory collapses into Nozick's. It is thus worth noting that Rawls has always argued that personal property is covered by the liberty principle, but investment capital is not. Rawls thinks of property rights as existing only *after* they have been established by whatever rules the theory of justice sets; writers like Nozick think of property rights as primordial. The right to some sorts of property, that is, those essential to self-expression and the preservation of intimate life, rests on considerations of liberty; those which sustain investment and impersonal sorts of economic activity are covered by the difference principle. Whether what architects are concerned with falls under the one heading or the other is interestingly debatable; the developer proposing to erect Riverside South is plainly a capitalist, and the drapes I hang in the windows of one of his apartments are plainly personal, but what we ought to say about people who buy houses and flats in the hope of capital appreciation as well as accommodation is another matter.

Rawlsian justice ought in principle to be visible in urban operation, in the sense that one would expect to be able to decipher a city's commitment to Rawlsian justice by inspecting the local income distribution and the life chances of its residents. Inequalities—other than minor and accidental ones—in the amenities of urban life and access to them violate Rawlsian justice *unless* we can demonstrate that they are the minimum inequalities required for the well-being of the least favored, and that the least favored are as well off as a representative worst-off group could be made. I say something more, in due course, about the range of things that "amenities" and "access" must cover, but I should give warning that Rawls's theory must raise questions about political institutions, educational arrangements, and access to whatever cultural opportunities people need.

Toronto might suggest an example of a city where Rawlsian justice is taken seriously. It has benefitted from a metropolitan plan that has concentrated very explicitly and energetically on *not* abandoning any group of the citizenry or any area of the city to the vagaries of market forces. I do not want to suggest that the Ontario government or any of the local governments under its surveillance have debated the question of what vision of a just society to pursue and have bought into Rawls. It is suggestive that the recent Toronto self-study should have focused on the question of what counts as a *healthy* city rather than on the perhaps narrower question of economic justice within the metropolitan area. In *Theory of Justice,* Rawls ended his discussion of justice by connecting his then egalitarian vision with the health of society conceived as a social union of social unions, or one might say a community of communities. Justice, it was easy to feel, had been folded into an account of the blessings of a society in which equality of mutual regard was a sustaining principle.

Turning back to justice, more narrowly conceived, I suggest that Rawls made such an impact on political theorists because so many of us have a rough and ready attachment to the "minimax" conception of justice, or to something closely related. Many of us begin with the thought that society ought to establish a baseline provision below which people can expect not to drop, and under pressure we then move this up to the thought that if we can raise the worst off above the level of that baseline without unduly worsening other people's position, we should do so. This is not exactly Rawls's 1971 view, since he refused to allow the trade-off envisaged here between losses for the better off and gains for the worse off. The point rather is that this form of justice—"baseline plus" and biased toward the benefits going to the worse off—is an egalitarian, patterned, nonhistorical account of the demands of justice in the spirit of Rawls's theory and is antipathetic to Nozickian and Hayekian ideas.

Common sense justice, like Rawlsian justice, seeks to do what Nozickian justice does not—that is, to override the arbitrary distribution of natural talent and inherited resources. To an even greater extent than Nozickian justice, Rawlsian justice is skeptical of the role of desert in the theory of justice. There is room for a rather thin concept of desert in the sense that we are only entitled to the rewards of a position by doing whatever it takes to qualify for it; but the theory of justice holds that positions ought to be established in a way that arranges positions of advantage for the benefit of the least favored, not so that they reflect desert. It would be difficult business to create a distributive system that reflected desert; what one might want to notice is that the public is very much attached to desert and that it is politically unwise to implement a distributive system that too flagrantly violates everyday conceptions of desert.

Utilitarian Justice

A third view derives justice from overall well-being. This is the utilitarian view of justice that almost every philosophical text attacks. Philosophers who set out to criticize it are prone to claim that utilitarianism provides the most widely held of all accounts of justice. This strikes me as implausible. What is

more plausible is that most people are in a rough and ready way consequen-
tialists; they think that *fiat justitia et pereat mundus* is extravagant. And they
think it proper to ask what benefit justice yields a society. The view that the
proper answer takes the form it takes in the arguments of Mill or Bentham is
not widely held. Still, it is not implausible to suggest that justice is a branch
of utility; what this means is that the distribution of resources and outcomes
within a city or region is just when it enhances overall well-being and unjust
when it does not.

What the governments of cities and regions ought to aim for is even so not
wholly clear: some utilitarianisms suggest it is *total* welfare, others that it is
maximum average welfare. With a fixed population these are the same thing
and other considerations have to be brought in to decide whether—as most
people intuitively believe—it matters how welfare is distributed. (Let house
prices stand in for welfare: Is it better that ten people own houses worth
$300,000 or that five own houses worth $150,000 and five own houses
worth $450,000? Does it matter if we know that the pleasures of ownership
are linear—the $450,000 house yields exactly three times the pleasure a
$150,000 house does?) The *total* conception pulls apart from the *maximum
average* when population varies; we can increase the total welfare within the
district under our control by admitting people as long as they are at least
happy to be alive.

Interestingly enough, this argument, whether or not it is an argument
about justice, is one that cities, regions, states, and nations all encounter.
New York in the 1880s seemed to many of its inhabitants to be a city facing
the choice between total welfare and average welfare: the city could try to
keep out immigrants in order to keep up the average standard of living, or let
them in and increase the total welfare. In general, regions wondering whether
to let in refugees, considering changes in welfare arrangements that might attract poor newcomers, and so on, face these arguments.

I do not mean that they always face them with principles that have a utilitarian provenance (directly at least); the more usual thought is that those
who are already here have rights that trump or at least weigh against those of
would-be immigrants. These belong more naturally in a schema like Nozick's. If "we" own all the resources locally available, we may do what we
choose with them; and if we want to keep out newcomers or run a particularly inhospitable welfare system, that is within our rights. In practice, it
seems to me, the public and politicians both work with a mixed bag of principles; the rights of incumbent populations are taken for granted but may
give way in whole or in part if the welfare gains are high enough. Even in a

utilitarian perspective a surrogate of such rights may enter through the back door, so to speak; without believing in the *rights* of incumbents, we may still see that there is a problem in managing the resentments of the prior arrivals and the needs of the newcomers in a welfare maximizing fashion, and plainly one way to do that is to filter the arrivals so as to minimize the cost to the already present citizenry.

Egalitarian Justice

Lastly—or penultimately—what one might call egalitarian, social-democratic justice is distinguishable from these three views. The thought behind this view of justice is quite difficult to spell out, for all its intuitive appeal. It is the thought that—negatively—nobody is so superior to anyone else that he or she deserves to do more than *somewhat* better than they. "How much" better is then a matter of continuous argument and negotiation; this is commonly backed by the positive thought that benefits ought to compensate people for the burdens they have borne or the handicaps they have labored under. Rawls's theory of justice is very much in this mold, and is in many ways a social-democratic rather than a liberal theory. What pulls egalitarian, social-democratic justice away from other views of the subject is that the idea that society ought to aim for a moral solidarity is inconsistent with extreme inequality of condition. The thought is a simple one: if society is in part a mutual assurance scheme for protection against the hazards of nature and the quasi-natural hazards presented by the unexpected effects of social cooperation, such as economic depressions, inflation, lead-poisoning, displacement for highway schemes, and so indefinitely on, justice is in part a matter of preserving the sentiment that "we're all in this together." The way to preserve the sentiment is to make the belief underlying it true. In this vein, considerations of justice are very difficult to keep entirely distinct from considerations of mutual regard, thoughts about the sort of fair play proper to quasi-familial relations, and ideal considerations about the sort of community that individuals would wish to belong to.

A Coda

The last consideration I should pick up is a point I have touched on before; in many areas, justice-as-desert is important—when awarding literary prizes, medals for gallantry, long-service awards for teachers and janitors, and so on. These considerations do not seem apt to questions of urban planning; the idea that everyone should have the services they deserve, no more and no less, is hard to do much with, as is the thought that they should live where they deserve in just the accommodation they deserve. But, there are two ways in which the concept of desert comes back into the discussion. One is via the thought that undeserved misfortune is properly something against which we are entitled to expect a measure of public defense; the other is that the benefits of urban government ought not to favor the undeserving who have brought misfortune upon themselves over the more deserving who are victims of bad luck. The allocation of public housing, for instance, can cause great resentment if it seems to violate that requirement.

Government and Free Association

Lastly, then, I make a few remarks about the embodiment of these ideas in urban life. The first thought is that questions of justice raise two issues about governance. This is particularly important in this context: philosophers are excessively prone to discuss justice as though some governmental machine stands ready to implement whatever favored conception of justice we come up with, save when they are explicitly interested in the legitimacy of government where their besetting weakness is to write as though a constitutional convention is in permanent session. Conversely, planners are prone to write as though everything in the city and region rotates around their own subject matter. I hope this excursus into theories of justice will raise the question of the appropriate economic unit of analysis; one question is whether suburbanites *owe* any duties of justice to the city they have left. Another is whether there is a discrepancy between where power lies and where the chips fall. New York City's problems with dependency on a less than friendly state government are familiar; less obvious is the fact that the "megalopolis" region now occupies a substantial portion of three states but has few common institutions.

It is obvious enough that the adjustment of authority to problems is anything but easy. Many failures of city government occur because the forces that dictate the welfare of urban inhabitants are regional or national: as witnessed by New York City's problems with its medical services, or its vulnerability to uncontrollable influxes of immigration for which no corresponding budgetary resources come on stream. Conversely, many problems are more local than the machinery intended to cope with them, and when local machinery is built it can go spectacularly wrong. Like all public education systems in the United States, New York City's has been reluctant to allow individual schools sufficient autonomy in matters of curriculum, promotion, and the use of resources generally, but when the sentiment for local (not school) autonomy gained ground in the late 1960s and local school districts were created, many of them swiftly became spectacularly corrupt and incompetent and remain so to this day.

All forms of community enhancement display the same difficulty, which is, after all, only what we should expect. There is no political system that can automatically ensure that each individual's pursuit of his or her own welfare will (by a visible or invisible hand) secure the common good and the welfare of all. Unless citizens think about collective goods and common interests and feel some obligation to promote them, they will not be promoted. The rise of community residents' associations (CRAs) reminds us that giving power to a group of residents to promote the interests of that district, or group of homeowners, can have two unlovely effects. One is that it will be oppressive to members—not an especially alarming issue if we are thinking of promoting CRA-like arrangements in public housing projects; the other is that it will set off a competitive struggle between different CRAs to hog the benefits and unload the costs onto their neighbors. Because currently the CRA phenomenon is visible in planned communities in the suburbs and in "adult communities" set up to protect the over-55s from the presence and the expense of other people's children, it mostly adds to the problems described immediately below. But one current trend is that of bringing back into the city some features of successful suburban life—the creation of "defensible space" for instance—in an attempt to rescue local communities. This is for the most part a benign and sensible exercise, but it brings with it the usual danger of setting community against community.

At present, the more obvious problem is the shift in power and resources to the suburbs. In the absence of adequate regional authorities this creates a danger that suburban voters (let alone upstate voters) will systematically shortchange the city on which the suburb depends. This might have any number of results. An obvious one is that it is a process that feeds on itself. As the diligent, well-organized, well-behaved, solidly married and provident leave the city for the suburb, the suburb will have increasing resources and fewer calls on them, while the city will be left with fewer resources and increasing calls. A non-solidaristic view of the world exacerbates the problem, since it is manifestly not true that city and suburb are all in it together. The end result of such a self-sustaining process is hard to predict. One view is that the selfish suburban voter is self-destructive: the city provides the suburb's reason for existence, and is the home of the headquarters of its economic life, so that a dying city will eventually destroy the suburb too. Another is that this is implausible; the future lies with the "edge city," a sort of circular ring around an empty center, where the various bits of development, linked by freeways, provide everything that a real city might provide—except urban life.

A second point is the less familiar one that access to power is one of the things that must be included among the resources with which distributive justice is concerned. This is not unfamiliar in theoretical discussions of forms of national government; democracy is commonly justified in terms of the justice of each affected person having some say in the rules and procedures that govern his or her affairs. A vote is a resource. This isn't a high-flown thought: political access in the sense of being able to pick up the phone and knowing your local representative will be on the other end is one of the things that political lobbyists treasure. It is less familiar in the form that I want to suggest we might think of it: that the political life of the city is itself a benefit, and not only in instrumental terms. That is, one of the things that a city can offer that suburban life cannot is the sense of a collective destiny in the hands of the urban community. To fit this thought into accounts of urban justice is not particularly difficult.

The accounts of justice I have sketched are formalistic as they stand. They rely on our having an intuitive idea of what is at stake, but they do not themselves provide an account of the "benefits" and "resources." They suggest a spectrum of possibilities from the planless utopia of Nozick's work through a more managed regime in Rawls, to a European or Canadian social-democratic mildly collectivist regime in the egalitarian vision. (I do not mean that there are not other sorts of collectivism; one might imagine that someone who hankered after the political virtue and political solidarity of the Roman republic would hanker after its architecture, too.) To add that forms of governance and forms of urban planning will also make a difference to their sense of themselves as political entities adds a complication but does not change the argument. Given the view of justice we find plausible, we can then think what cities and regions do better and what they do worse, or more likely, find ourselves facing the familiar task of balancing their successes along one dimension against their failures along another. The utilitarian theory of justice would, as with every other aspect of utilitarianism, have to wait upon the facts to side with Los Angeles and *laissez-faire* or Toronto and humanitarian regional planning, though it does not take much imagination to guess which way the facts will push. But Hayek always argued that a *laissez-faire* economy would in fact achieve what Rawls's *Theory of Justice* proposed—

the "best-off worst-off" among competing economic systems—so it is not peculiar to utilitarianism that it must wait before it pronounces.

Crucially, however, theories of justice take on a distinctive character as we fill our conceptions of what the city has to offer. We need not share Marx's contempt for "the idiocy of rural life" to believe that the city's riches are not only material but intellectual and cultural; this means not only the possibility of good public schooling that can specialize in a diversity of different fields, but the provision of art galleries and museums, concert halls, the beautification of public buildings, and the maintenance of the built environment as something that enhances existence rather than presenting a constant affront to the sensibilities. *Justice* in this context is the question of how access to all these things is distributed: whether the quality of schools depends excessively on the wealth of the neighborhood, whether public libraries are notably thin on the ground in the poorer districts, whether theaters cluster in one small district. This is not to deny that employment, on the one hand, and basic services such as health care, police, water, sewerage, and lighting, on the other, are equally and perhaps more important. A theory of justice, however, must in the end rest on a view both of what constitutes the goods of association, and which of them can be or should be provided by, or with the aid and encouragement of government. Thus, Nozick's "buy it if you want it" approach would seem to rule out government action in these areas, while Rawls's utilitarianism and egalitarianism would allow it but on different bases and in different amounts.

This leads me to a speculative finale. I have said that we cannot simply *see* whether a city implements justice; in a Nozickian universe, this is a deep and basic truth; in other universes, it only means that there is much else we need to know besides the state of the housing stock, employment rates, and expenditures on social services. But it might be thought that a city *ought* to display its sense of itself as a community—or if its sentiments are not so much communal as national or global, its sense of itself, period. This need not be a unitary conception: New York City conceives of itself as simultaneously the capital of the world and an offshoot of Guandong, Palermo, and who knows where else. The attempt also raises difficult questions about how we can strengthen neighborhoods without weakening citywide loyalties, and vice versa. But our idea of the city ought to be a participatory conception; sharing in it is one of the gifts a city can offer.

Readers accustomed to the thought that urban planning is dependent on political struggles that share the roughness of most political activity may think that to speculate in this way is Pollyannaish—that it presupposes what is not true, that principle can guide our actions in these matters. The reply is twofold: public and group pressure is shaped by principles, however inchoate and incoherent people may sound when asked about them, and it is the task of political leaders to try to shape opinion in a principled direction; it is easier to do if one has some understanding of what principles there are in the public arena. We may not want philosopher kings, in the high Platonic mode, but we might, in the low Rortyian mode, want them for PR and something a little better.

From the Environmentally Challenged City to the Ecological City

John Spengler and Tim Ford

Urban areas around the world are ecologically unbalanced, and most are environmentally challenged. In the developing world, urban areas are increasing in population at a rate faster than can be accommodated by the infrastructure of housing, schools, hospitals, and roads. As a result, many of the urban areas around the world have an undernourished, unemployed, and inadequately sheltered underclass. By 2025 the urban population in the developing world will be four times that of developed countries. Nearly all of the world's rapidly expanding cities are in poorer countries and nearly half of these cities' populations live in extreme deprivation.

In contrast, cities of the developed countries appear to provide municipal amenities of a safe water supply, clean air, waste removal, transport, health services, and public housing. Looks can be deceiving. Concerning environmental quality, more than 25 years of federal and state action have shown dividends in improved air quality, safer drinking water, and more thorough waste water treatment. But should those of us living in North American and Western European cities feel sanguine about our environmental quality? Not quite. With the growth in population, number of vehicles, and miles traveled, energy demands are not keeping pace with engineering controls that have been the underpinnings of environmental management strategies. There is a growing recognition that local and global environments are under increased stress (U.S. EPA 1995). Industrial cities are in decline or are undergoing transformation in the post-industrial era. However, poorer classes continue to migrate to the new economically depressed centers of cities.

The issues that threaten all of our futures are sustainability of terrestrial ecosystems; total air pollution loadings; contaminants in food and water; and health of the oceans. The urbanization of the world's population along with economic expansion and resource consumption exacerbate these stressors. One lesson taught by our environmental history is that a failure to consider the consequences of social, economic, and technological changes may impose substantial—and avoidable—economic and environmental costs on future generations (U.S. EPA 1995).

Air Quality

Air pollution is a complex mixture of gases and particles that originate from combustion, abrasion, and evaporation. Fuel combustion for electrical power generation, transportation, and industry are the primary sources of sulfur dioxides (SO_2), nitrogen dioxide (NO_2), carbon monoxide (CO), and particles. These pollutants along with evaporation of hydrocarbons from mobile, stationary, and natural sources lead to photochemical smog and many toxic air pollutants. The criteria pollutants (SO_2, NO_2, CO, ozone, lead, and particles) are considered community air pollutants because their sources are widely distributed and virtually the entire population is exposed to these pollutants to some extent. Effective control of these community pollutants requires almost nationwide emission standards, clean fuel requirements, and mobile source controls at the point of manufacturing. As a result of federal and state control programs, many urban areas have substantially cleaner air now than just 10 or 20 years ago. However, as we recognize and measure the progress, we should be cognizant that health effects for exposure to CO, SO_2, ozone, lead, and particles have been documented at levels below our current standards set to protect the public.

The quality of outdoor air is monitored regularly across the country. Sites are located primarily in and around urban areas or where there is major industry. The U.S. Environmental Protection Agency (EPA) archives air pollution data and annually updates trends in emissions and ambient air pollution. The most recent status report in 1993, shows that 59 million Americans reside in areas that still exceed federal health standards (Figure 1). As of September 1994, there were 93 urban areas in nonattainment of the ozone (O_3) standard, 38 in nonattainment of the CO standard, and 83 in nonattainment of the particulate standard (PM_{10}) (Table 1).

Violations for these three pollutants illustrate the complexity of the air pollution problem. Carbon monoxide comes primarily from automobiles; more than 90% of CO emissions in most urban areas are from cars. Although today's cars are 95% cleaner on average than the cars built before 1970, and

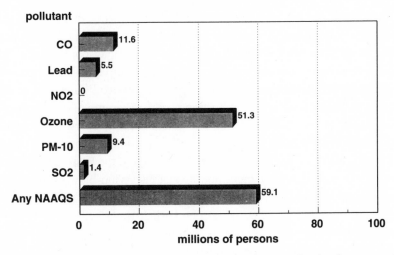

Figure 1. Number of persons living in countries with air quality levels not meeting the primary NAAQS in 1993 (based on 1990 population data and 1993 air quality data). *Source:* U.S. EPA (1994).

Table 1. Nonattainment Areas for NAAQS Pollutants as of September 1994

Pollutant	Number of Nonattainment Areas[a]
Carbon monoxide (CO)	38
Lead (Pb)	13
Nitrogen dioxide (NO_2)	1
Ozone (O_3)	93
Particulate matter (PM_{10})	83
Sulfur dioxide (SO_2)	47

[a]Unclassified areas are not included in the totals.
Source: U.S. EPA (1994).

there has been a 15% reduction in CO emissions between 1984 and 1993, vehicle miles traveled by Americans (now exceeding 2,000 billion miles each year) have steadily increased. The increased number of cars congests urban streets, lowers speed, and increases fuel consumption, further compounding CO problems.

It is important to recognize that particle pollution originates from a variety of sources and, therefore, that the composition varies greatly. Particles in the less than 10 μm size range are readily inhaled and the mass concentrations in this size range have been associated with health effects. Particles less than 1 μm in size are primarily comprised of combustion products, carbon, poly-aromatic hydrocarbons, sulfates, and many low-boiling-point metals. The large size fraction, 1 μm to 10 μm, is typically made up of resuspended earth crustal material, natural organic debris, pollens, tire/road fragments, and, at times, soot fallout from poor combustion facilities. Because of the diversity of sources contributing to the different size ranges of PM_{10} (coarse and fine fractions), different parts of the country will have different problems. Wood burning in the mountain states, both in the West and the East, can fill valleys with smoke during winter nighttime inversions. Wind-blown dust in arid areas is responsible for many of the particulate matter (PM_{10}) violations. Heavy industry and even heavy auto and truck traffic will cause localized concentrations that exceed standards. Figure 2 shows the areas of the United States designated as nonattainment for PM_{10}.

Because more than 80% of the nation's SO_2 emissions originate from utilities with tall stacks in the states bordering and to the east of the Mississippi River, sulfate particles, including acid aerosols, make up a substantial fraction (about 30%) of the PM_{10} mass in the eastern United States. Figure 3 displays the concentrations of sulfate particles as simulated contours on a map of the United States. The area along the western Appalachians and into western and central Pennsylvania experiences high sulfate deposition and acidity of rain and aerosols. As sulfur dioxide emissions are reduced by 50% (10 million tons/year) over the next 5 to 10 years, reductions of fine particle sulfates are expected (Spengler et al. 1990; Office of Technology Assessment 1985).

The Clean Air Act Amendments (CAAA) of 1990 set our nation on a course to meet the criteria air pollutants standards. To accomplish compliance, many states are required to revise their control strategies: lower emissions limits for existing and new sources, and a sweeping set of transportation strategies aimed at encouraging cleaner fuels, low or zero emission vehicles, and enhanced inspection and maintenance. For many urban areas it is clear that even these approaches will not be sufficient to meet the requirements of the CAAA and avoid federal sanctions. Vehicle miles must be reduced by restricting parking, raising tolls and fees, and requiring linkage to public transportation for new development.

Public enthusiasm for environmental protection involving control strategies that alter fuels, require broad participation, and restrict discretionary movement is vaporous. There already has been a public backlash against government interference into private decisions in Alaska, Maine, New Jersey, and Michigan. Politicians in these states are openly defying the EPA. Alternatives

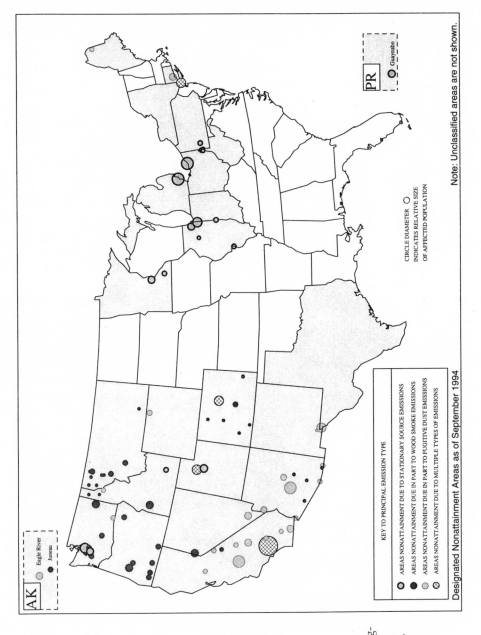

Figure 2. Areas designated nonattainment for PM$_{10}$ particulates, by emission type. *Source:* U.S. EPA (1994).

AK

Eagle River
Juneau

KEY TO PRINCIPAL EMISSION TYPE

○ AREAS NONATTAINMENT DUE TO STATIONARY SOURCE EMISSIONS
● AREAS NONATTAINMENT DUE IN PART TO WOOD SMOKE EMISSIONS
◉ AREAS NONATTAINMENT DUE IN PART TO FUGITIVE DUST EMISSIONS
⊗ AREAS NONATTAINMENT DUE TO MULTIPLE TYPES OF EMISSIONS

CIRCLE DIAMETER ○
INDICATES RELATIVE SIZE
OF AFFECTED POPULATION

Designated Nonattainment Areas as of September 1994

PR

○ Guaynabo

Note: Unclassified areas are not shown.

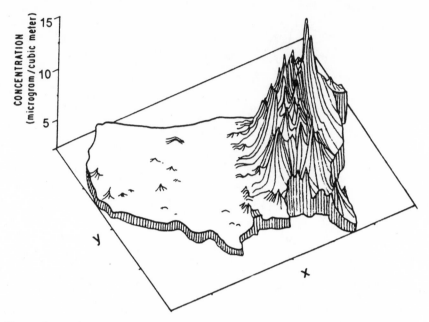

Figure 3. Predicted annual sulfate concentrations in 1990 from the Brookhaven long-distance transport model. Emissions are from major coal-burning facilities and include area sources. Sulfate concentrations (in µg/m³) are proportional to altitude and are spatially averaged over 32 × 32-km grids (x,y).

to "command and control" environmental management might be better received. The technology of remote or noninvasive sampling of tailpipe emissions is proving a reliable way to identify a much smaller fraction of the fleet that has abnormally high emissions. In a recent *Science* article, Beaton et al. (1995) describe the results of indirect tailpipe sensing and the currently mandated methods. Figure 4 shows the distribution of emissions for a set of vehicles that were more or less randomly monitored. The article authors argue that since the public at large benefits from cleaner air, it should be willing to subsidize the cost for repair of faulty emission systems or the retirement of offending vehicles.

Many other, more innovative strategies include telecommuting, restricting vehicle use, staggered work times, creation of no-vehicle zones, and reducing the volatile organic compound content in consumer products, among others. Developers and urban planners will have to integrate designs with environmental objectives.

Many air pollution health studies conducted over the last ten years have

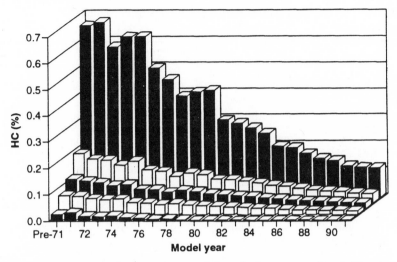

Figure 4. Average HC exhaust emissions of the vehicles measured in California, reported as the HC percentage equivalent to propane and corrected for water and any excess air present in the exhaust. The emissions for each model year were sorted and divided into five groups (quintiles). The average emissions of the five quintiles for each model year are plotted from front to back, lowest to highest. Pre-71 includes all 1970 and older vehicles. *Source:* Beaton et al. (1995).

consistently shown adverse health responses at exposure levels below our current standards. National Air Quality Standards for PM_{10}, ozone, and carbon monoxide provide no margin of safety. For each pollutant, a substantial fraction of our population is susceptible.

Tables 2 and 3 summarize studies that associate ambient particulate pollution with daily mortality and hospital admissions for urban populations. These studies and several others published more recently (Pope et al. 1995; Dockery et al. 1993) consistently show this relationship between particulate pollution and illness and early deaths. There are important implications that particle pollution at current levels is causing morbidity and shortening lives. If 3% of the mortality (50,000 deaths per year) is caused by air pollution, primarily from fossil fuels, our society is confronted with a serious dilemma. "No safe levels" require policymakers, and the public as well, to look anew at our goals for environmental quality. We can expect that adverse health effects are occurring in every urban area whether standards are exceeded or not.

These recent studies (Pope et al. 1995; Dockery et al. 1993) provide us with a powerful planning tool—the quantification of an exposure–response relationship. The impacts of new sources, control strategies, electric power

Table 2. Recent Time-Series Studies of Effects of Particulates on Daily Mortality

Reference	Particulate Measure Used in the Study[a]	Percent Increase in Mortality for a 10 µg/m³ Increase in Daily PM_{10}[b]	Study Location
Schwartz and Dockery (1992a)	Total suspended particulates	1.2% ± 0.2	Philadelphia, PA
Schwartz (1991)	Total suspended particulates	1.0% ± 0.3	Detroit, MI
Schwartz and Dockery (1992b)	Total suspended particulates	0.7% ± 0.2	Steubenville, OH
Schwartz (1993)	PM_{10}	1.0% ± 0.4	Birmingham, AL
Dockery et al. (1992)	PM_{10}	1.5% ± 0.7	St. Louis, MO
Pope et al. (1992)	PM_{10}	1.5% ± 0.3	Utah Valley, UT
Fairley (1990)	Coefficient of haze	0.8% ± 0.4	Santa Clara County, CA
Özkaynak and Kinney (1995)	Coefficient of haze[c]	0.8% ± 0.3	New York City, NY
Kinney and Özkaynak (1991)	KM	0.4% ± 0.1	Los Angeles, CA
Özkaynak et al. (1993)	Total suspended particulates	0.6% ± 0.2	Toronto, Canada

[a]Conversions used: $0.55 \times TSP = PM_{10}$; $Sulfates/0.25 = PM_{10}$; $2.2 \times KM = PM_{10}$; $COH/0.55 = PM_{10}$.

[b]Plus or minus one standard error.

[c]$40 \times COH = PM_{10}$.

Source: Özkaynak (1993).

Table 3. Recent Studies of Acute Effects of Particles on Hospital Admissions

Study	Particulate Measure Used in the Study[a]	Percent Increase in Admissions for a 10 µg/m^3 Increase in Daily PM_{10}[b]	Study Location
Thurston et al. (1992)	Sulfates	Asthma: 2.1% ± 1.4 Total respiratory: 2.2% ± 0.4	Buffalo, NY
Thurston et al. (1992)	Sulfates	Asthma: 1.9% ± 0.7 Total respiratory: 1.0% ± 0.4	New York City, NY
Özkaynak et al. (1990)	Total suspended particulates	Pneumonia and influenza for <15 year olds: 15% ± 0.4	Boston, MA
Burnett et al. (1993)	Sulfates	Total respiratory: 1.0% ± 0.2	Southern Ontario, Canada
Thurston et al. (1993)	$PM_{2.5}$	Asthma: 2.2% ± 1.6 Total respiratory: 3.6% ± 1.6	Toronto, Canada

[a]Conversions used: Sulfates/0.25 = PM_{10}; 0.55 × TSP = PM_{10}; $PM_{2.5}$/0.60 = PM_{10}.
[b]Plus or minus one standard error.
Source: Özkaynak (1993).

demand, and transportation policies, among others, can now be quantified. Development can be evaluated in terms of the additional particle pollution and hence its health consequences. We will either have to agree on acceptable risk or require new development to offset projected impacts by reducing and trading off emissions, exposures, or calculated risk elsewhere.

Similarly, analyses of hospital admissions and daily death records show a strong statistical relationship to ozone concentrations. These studies, summarized in Tables 4 and 5, have been done in Los Angeles, New York, Toronto, and elsewhere. It is significant that findings were consistent across these cities even though there are substantial differences in frequency and level of ozone concentrations.

Other studies (Holquin et al. 1985; Whittemore and Korn 1980) have shown that the likelihood of an asthmatic child experiencing an attack or shortness of breath or requiring medication increases as ambient ozone increases. Consistent with these findings are the results of chamber studies of

Table 4. Recent Studies of Acute Effects of Ozone on Hospital Admissions

Study	Percent Increase in Admissions for a 50-ppb Increase in Daily Maximum 1-hr Ozone[a]	Study Location
Thurston et al. (1992)	Asthma: 16% ± 7.0 Total respiratory: 12% ± 7.0	Buffalo, NY
Thurston et al. (1992)	Asthma: 9% ± 3.5 Total respiratory: 4% ± 1.5	New York City, NY
Özkaynak et al. (1990)	Pneumonia and influenza for >15 year olds: 20% ± 5.0	Boston, MA
Burnett et al. (1993)	Total respiratory: 6% ± 1.5	Southern Ontario, Canada
Thurston et al. (1993)	Asthma: 16% ± 7.0 Total respiratory: 19% ± 7.0	Toronto, Canada

[a]Plus or minus one standard error.
Source: Özkaynak (1993).

Table 5. Recent Time-Series Studies of Effects of Ozone on Daily Total Mortality

Study	Percent Increase in Daily Mortality for a 50-ppb Increase in Daily Maximum 1-hr Ozone[a]	Study Location
Kinney and Özkaynak (1991)	1.2% ± 0.3	Los Angeles, CA
Özkaynak and Kinney (1995)	1.5% ± 0.5	New York City, NY
Özkaynak et al. (1993)	2.2% ± 0.8	Toronto, Canada

[a]Plus or minus one standard error.
Source: Özkaynak (1993).

controlled human exposures (McDonnell et al. 1991) and summer camp studies (Raizenne and Spengler 1989). Both types of investigations reveal that pulmonary function is impaired proportionally to ozone exposure and exercise rate. A subset of the population appears to have quite reactive airways that are up to five times more responsive.

Recommendations for reducing urban air pollution are as follow:

1. The regional nature of transported particles, ozone precursors, and acid rain call for new strategies beyond local and state control programs. The densely populated eastern seaboard is an example where coordinated interstate programs are needed to control ozone precursors that cause violations from Richmond, Virginia, to Bar Harbor, Maine.

2. Health effects are experienced at levels well below current standards. Further reduction of particulates and other pollutants will require new strategies that incorporate the trading of emissions and trading of risk.

3. Over 3,000 chemical substances have been identified in urban air. Yet routine monitoring is very sparse and the number of compounds assessed is limited. The network needs to be expanded because new evidence suggests that some of these chemicals may contribute to endocrine disruption, immunologic disorders, respiratory disease, birth defects, and cancer.

4. Virtually everything we know about urban exposures to air pollution is derived from fixed-location ambient monitors. There is a great need to understand personal exposures so populations at differential risk and the sources contributing to risk can be identified. New management strategies can be devised that are more cost-effective at reducing risk once we have accurately apportioned the contributors to risk.

Water Quality

The quantity and quality of freshwater, nationally and internationally, has been defined as being in a state of crisis (Gleick 1993). Of course, water is not distributed evenly across the surface of the globe. For example, in North America there is extreme inequity between Southern California and the Pacific Northwest. Where the water supply is inadequate, the resource is limited by pollution. This results in the need for extensive and costly water treatment, and in many cases even this is not sufficient to guarantee the safety of our drinking water. Even within developed countries we are seeing alarming

increases in waterborne disease, with cryptosporidiosis outbreaks directly
traced to drinking water supplies (MacKenzie et al. 1994). In addition, epidemiological evidence suggests that many other infectious diseases can be
waterborne, including the spread of *Helicobacter pylori* (Klein et al. 1991), the
organism implicated in the formation of gastric and duodenal ulcers.

There are three critical areas that warrant concern: source water quality
(and quantity), water treatment practices, and water distribution. At each
stage, from source to consumer, there is potential for both microbiological
and chemical contamination of drinking water. The greater the volume consumed, the greater the risks for the following reasons: relatively clean source
waters may become limited and less pristine sources will be utilized; treatment facilities may be overwhelmed by demand; and excessive wastewater
production may place source waters and leaking distribution systems at
greater risk.

South Florida may be one of the worst offenders in the United States due
to excessive consumption. Many towns are reported to have water consumption rates more than ten times higher per capita than the national average
(Duplaix 1990). Florida has compounded the problem through past mistakes
in water management practices originally designed for flood control. These
practices have resulted in channelization of much of Florida's water systems.
This has dramatically changed both the ecology and the hydrological cycle of
southern Florida. The result is drastically reduced rates of aquifer recharge.
In addition, reclamation of wetlands for agriculture has not only removed
species' habitats but also the natural cleansing capacity of the marshes. Re-
sultant pollution to Lake Okeechobee and the Everglades, for example, is
having dramatic consequences for the environment and, eventually, human
health (Duplaix 1990).

Responsible resource management is critical to protect our water sources.
Most of our surface waters are contaminated to varying extents. There are
very few streams, rivers, or lakes that could be declared free of *Giardia,* a protozoan pathogen that until recently was the primary cause of identified waterborne disease outbreaks in the United States. This is partly because of the
ubiquity of the organisms in wildlife. Giardia has recently been replaced by
Cryptosporidium as the major cause of waterborne disease. *Cryptosporidium*
was the cause of diarrheal disease that has been estimated to have afflicted
400,000 residents of Milwaukee in March 1993 (MacKenzie et al. 1994).
These protozoan pathogens can be fatal to an immunologically compromised
population. Cattle are the primary carriers of *Cryptosporidium* and many of

the nation's water sources are surrounded by diary farms. One of the best known examples is New York's water supply in the Catskills (Wapner 1993).

Groundwater has traditionally been viewed as a pristine water source. Wastewaters are thought to be cleansed by natural microbial and sorptive processes as they percolate through soils. We have removed much of the top-soil through agriculture and development, and we frequently exceed the carrying capacity of the soils with nonbiodegradable pollutants. It is not surprising then to note that it is estimated that 1 million gallons of noxious liquid from old, leaking landfills seeps into Florida's water table each day (Duplaix 1990). Groundwaters are not unlimited resources. Deep aquifers are replenished very slowly and may have been generated by ice ages and on a geologic time scale. The Ogallala aquifer that transformed the central plains of the United States into a fertile agricultural area is being replenished at 5% of the rate it is being extracted (Zwingle 1993). *National Geographic* reports that Texas may use up two-thirds of their supply by the year 2020 (Zwingle 1993). Whether the supply is surface water or groundwater, our management strategies have inevitably resulted in a diminishing, more polluted resource.

Development of water treatment in the early part of this century completely changed public health in the developed countries. However, we are seeing an increasing trend among microbes to develop strategies to survive water treatment and disinfection. For example, the protozoan pathogens mentioned above form chlorine-resistant cysts. Milwaukee's treatment plants, which included filtration, were in complete compliance with the law before and throughout the cryptosporidiosis outbreak (Kaminiski et al. 1994). Federal guidelines have been improved since then, but it is unclear whether they are yet sufficient (Kaminiski et al. 1994).

Regulations in the United States require utilities to install filtration if source waters cannot meet specific standards of quality. However, there is a serious concern with distribution of this treated water. Why build an extremely expensive water treatment facility if the distribution system is essentially disintegrating beneath the city? Many of the systems are old. In Boston sections of pipe are estimated to be over 100 years old. Sections of pipe run contiguous with sewer lines and in some cases may even be routed within sewers. In addition, old corroded systems may have many potential interconnections with sewer lines. This is an increasing problem in rapidly expanding cities worldwide. Distribution system replacement programs are extremely costly and very slow to be implemented. Even given a relatively modern and presumably sound distribution system, there is an inherent problem in its use. Severe pressure drops from legal use of fire hydrants, illegal use of hydrants by contractors, and increasing pressure from high-rise buildings all contribute to the potential for back-siphoning of contaminants into the system.

The risk of contamination is high in distribution systems, whether caused by a fault at the treatment plant, interconnections, or misuse of hydrants. Hence, we maintain a disinfection residual within the system. However, this fluctuates, depending on initial dosage, monitoring efficiency, organic loading, distance from the treatment plant, and flow rate within the part of the system. Once contamination has occurred, chlorine-resistant "biofilms" form rapidly on pipe surfaces (Ford 1993). These biofilms provide a nutrient-rich environment for pathogens to survive and in some cases proliferate. Individual pathogens appear to be becoming more and more resistant to disinfection, or are developing strategies to avoid disinfection. *Legionella pneumophila,* the causative organism of legionellosis (Legionnaire's disease), is an excellent example of an organism that survives disinfection by essentially hiding inside protozoan cysts or within biofilms (Kramer and Ford 1994).

Recommendations for these water quality problems are as follow:

1. Education is necessary to limit water use and therefore reduce production of waste. An encouraging sample is the development of xeriscaping in Florida.

2. Ecologically sound technology is essential to avoid environmental degradation caused by impoundment of waters, channelization, excessive pumping of groundwaters, and so on.

3. Water resources need to be valued and usage should almost certainly be metered, while still providing public water supplies.

4. Considerable investment in distribution system design, including materials, water treatment techniques, and disinfection regimes, is necessary if we wish to avoid an increasing rate of waterborne disease outbreaks both in the United States and worldwide.

5. If the United States is to be considered a leader in the safety of drinking water, we must develop exportable technologies to the developing world. Removal of chlorinated disinfection by-products by expensive activated carbon filtration may be considered essential for some of the wealthier communities in the United States (ignoring the ethical considerations), but in regions of the world where life expectancies may be less than 50 years due to infectious disease, these technologies are not only irrelevant but potential economic disasters. Desalina-

tion is an option for oil-rich nations, but for many of the developing countries a low-technology answer, like slow-sand filtration, could essentially save or improve millions of lives.

Indoor Environments

People engage in many activities throughout a day and over their lives, with the majority of these occurring inside some built structure. Studies have shown that in excess of 90% of the time we are indoors and only 5% or less are we actually directly exposed to outdoor pollutants. Most of our indoor time is spent in our residence. It is reasonable that sources inside these indoor locations are important determinants of our exposures to fuels, tobacco smoke, pesticides, radon, fungi, mites, cat allergen, and chemical compounds.

The heating, cooling, and lighting of our built environment consumes about one-third of our energy. And now, internal heat loads in modern office buildings equipped with computers, printers, copiers, facsimile machines, and other equipment have further increased the requirements for air conditioning. But the foundation for problems with indoor environments was established when construction techniques began to change in the 1960s. Buildings began to be built with internal supporting frames of steel and reinforced concrete. The envelope of the building was fabricated off site to be hoisted and sealed in place. The internal climate of the modern building is now dependent on the design, operation, and maintenance of the mechanical ventilation system. To provide comfort for the occupants, the ventilation systems must cope with internal heat gain, struggle with sensible and radiative heat fluxes at the boundary, and have considerable dynamic range to meet variable weather conditions.

As more people have experienced artificial indoor environments, there has been a rise in dissatisfaction. Complaints related to the indoor climate in nonindustrial buildings have increased markedly for nearly two decades. In some cases the illness can be defined and related to specific environmental factors, such as allergens, combustion products, and irritating odors. In other cases a diffuse set of symptoms are reported, but no specific cause has been identified (ATS 1990; Cone and Hodgson 1989; Kreiss 1989). On the basis of this distinction, building-related health problems of known etiology are identified as building-related illness, whereas building-related health problems with no known etiology and without physical or laboratory findings are identified as sick- (or tight-) building syndrome.

Building-Related Illness

Symptoms of building-related illness include toxic, allergic, or infectious manifestations that can be identified by a physician and a clinical laboratory. At times, specific etiological agents can also be identified in the building in question. The types of building-related illness vary and include hypersensitivity pneumonitis, asthma, Legionnaire's disease, influenza, and carbon monoxide poisoning (ATS 1990; Hollowell and Miksch 1981; Kreiss 1989). Resolution of the problem typically involves removal of the source of the problem rather than increasing the ventilation. The incidence of building-related illness may be relatively low, and therefore it may easily be missed.

Sick-Building Syndrome

Sick-building syndrome has generally been identified when a substantial number of individuals in a particular building or a portion of the building complain of a diffuse but often common set of symptoms. These symptoms, though nonspecific in isolation, form a recognizable pattern that has been repeatedly observed in connection with sick-building syndrome (ATS 1990; Hodgson 1989; Kreiss 1989; Molhave 1987; WHO 1982). The common symptoms include eye, nose, and throat irritation, headache, recurrent fatigue, drowsiness or dizziness, and reduced powers of concentration (ATS 1990; Cone and Hodgson 1989; Molhave 1985, 1987; WHO 1982). The symptoms generally begin slowly and progress. They are related to the time spent at work. Most individuals report relief of symptoms on leaving the workplace and a recurrence on reentry.

Most documented cases of sick-building syndrome have been reported in newly constructed or newly remodeled energy-efficient buildings having a centrally controlled mechanical ventilation system. Such structures are almost always sealed, air-conditioned buildings that do not permit the windows to be opened (WHO 1982). Under these conditions a wide variety of pollutants may contaminate the indoor air (ATS 1990; Lebret et al. 1986; Molhave 1985; WHO 1982).

Sick-building syndrome has been attributed to a variety of conditions, including inadequate ventilation, presence of pollutants such as volatile organic compounds, moisture conditions related to humidification and chilling systems, biological contamination, or even outdoor contaminants brought in through the ventilation system (Burge et al. 1987; Finnegan et al. 1984; Kreiss 1989; Molhave 1985). Early investigations of sick-building syndrome often attributed the symptoms to mass hysteria. However, as the number of reports and outbreaks mounted, and as clinical and epidemiologic patterns emerged, attention was directed to searching for causal factors within the indoor air of problem buildings. British and Danish investigators have performed large epidemiologic studies of symptoms reported in relation to building characteristics. In some instances a specific cause was identified; in others none was discovered (Burge et al. 1987; Gammage and Kaye 1985; Spengler et al. 1982).

In a recent continuation of the Danish town hall studies, Gyntelberg et al. (1994) showed a significant correlation between the prevalence of gram-negative bacteria (the source of endotoxins) in indoor dust and general symptoms of fatigue, heavy headedness, headache, dizziness, and concentration problems, as well as symptoms from the mucous membranes of the upper respiratory tract.

As might be imagined, diagnosing and evaluating building-related problems can tax the abilities of even the most seasoned professional. At times building-related health problems are resolved easily and quickly through a discussion between the occupants and the building management. Under some circumstances, however, it becomes necessary to seek specialized consultation. Protocols that combine industrial hygiene and epidemiologic methods have been developed to study building-associated illnesses (ATS 1990; CIAQ 1987; Quinlan et al. 1989). This approach involves an interdisciplinary effort among health scientists, engineers, and architects. Protocols have been developed to examine heating, ventilation, and air-conditioning systems (ATS 1990; CIAQ 1987). Common problems in the operation of these systems are generally found in three areas: inadequate maintenance, load changes, and control modifications. Inadequate maintenance is reflected in such problems as missing or dirty filters, contaminated heating and cooling coils and drip pans, and disconnected exhaust fans. Load changes arise when the system is required to meet the needs of a higher occupant density, increased thermal demands (e.g., lighting and computers), or new sources of contaminants (e.g., copy machines and printers). Control-system problems may arise when, in a cost-cutting effort, the system is mistakenly adapted for a more simple operation (ATS 1990).

As the American work force becomes increasingly involved in the service sector rather than in manufacturing, the problem with buildings will take on an increased significance. Already, some 85 million people work in our nation's 4.5 million commercial and municipal structures. Further, it is likely that the population of potentially susceptible individuals is growing as women make up more of the work force, and there is a natural progression to an aging work force exacerbated by the removal of mandatory retirement. A more genetically diverse population is expected to manifest more symptoms.

While it is not known exactly how many of our nation's 4.5 million buildings experience health- and discomfort-related problems, some estimate that about one-third of the buildings are demonstrably "sick," while another one-third have flaws that given a particular set of circumstances could cause them to become "sick" buildings. When considering the size of the population at risk and the cost of medical care and lost productivity, it is somewhat surprising that the sick-building problem has not gained more recognition by the federal government. Evidence is mounting that the exposures in our homes, schools, workplaces, arenas, cars, buses, trains, and airplanes can result in a relative risk, substantially more than found outdoors or even in the vicinity of known Superfund waste sites. Radon, molds and allergens, environmental tobacco smoke, pesticides, and organic compound vapors coming from many indoor products offer ample evidence that forethought (measurements, design, and restrictions) would go a long way toward solving these problems that plague contemporary buildings.

Future City Environments

The world is under stress, growing in population by 90 million a year. We can expect a population of 10 billion in 2050. The population growth is greatest in the developing world, which currently consumes energy at one-tenth the annual rate of those of us living in countries with more developed economies. Yet the rapid expansion in economic growth in China, India, and elsewhere in Asia will double personal energy consumption for almost one-third of the world's population over the next ten years.

Much of the growth in populations will be in urban areas. By early in the 21st century there will be 65 urban areas with more than 4 million inhabitants. Fifty of these urban areas will be in developing nations. Environmental conditions in these urban areas are bad and will get worse. Factors that contribute to the worsening of environmental amenities are listed below.

1. The private sector of property owners, developers, and commerce are only marginally involved in setting priorities for growth and investment. The public sector exercises a near monopoly when it comes to setting policies and investing public resources.

2. Governments typically have a sector approach dealing in a fractured and uncoordinated way. Education, health services, housing, transportation, and commercial development are hardly ever coordinated around overarching goals.

3. Short-term thinking permeates much of governmental actions. This, in part, reflects electoral cycles and budget horizons.

4. The public resists change that is particular to an aging population fearing a diminished economy. Resistance to change starts with local neighborhoods but is extending to an abhorrence for any form of government intervention.

5. The psychological appeal of the car with independence, freedom, and expression is very strong. Efforts to force public transit ridership will be resisted unless done in a way that people feel they have freely chosen it as a preference.

6. We are enamored by technological solutions. In many respects, for example, water treatment or air pollution control measures for automobiles, environmental degradation is combatted with a heavy reliance on engineering. This overdependence on technology has relegated other approaches involving public persuasion, education, and ethics to fringe status.

7. Urban infrastructure and buildings do not have much flexibility to adapt to changing demands. Spatial patterns and structures are established by historic and economic interest. Demographics, property values, and environmental amenities, among other factors, change over time.

8. The costs of urban congestion are diffuse. Those who suffer the burden of lost productivity and frustration are not organized. They do not consider themselves as a special interest group and hence have no influence on a centralized public transportation or planning agency. Solutions, or at least investment in potential solutions, are dislocated from those who suffer the cost.

At a recent conference on Mexico City's environmental problems ("International Seminar on Urban Sustainability and Management of the Atmospheric Basis of the Federal District and the State of Mexico Metropolitan Area," Mexico City, May 22–25, 1995), Josef Konvitz of the Organization of Economic Cooperation and Development (OECD) presented a talk entitled "The Ecological City" in which he encouraged newly appointed federal officials to cast off the old paradigms because mega-cities are on their own. Solutions devised for Mexico City, or even other innovative attempts, will serve as global models. He outlined five principles that might bridge the processes.

1. All units of government must be involved. Incentives and sanctions have to be used because communities cannot be allowed not to play.

2. Land use is central to planning and can be used to accomplish other societal goals.

3. Life-cycle concepts of land use must consider alternative futures. Buildings have to be flexible. Development that projects a long half-life must link to services and relate to secondary development, including recreation and open space. This could provide incentives for long-term adaptability.

4. Transportation has to be considered as promoting productivity and directing land use. It is a planning tool that cannot be justified by conventional accounting methods and, therefore, has to be justified differently.

5. Include the public in the process of devising democratically effective solutions. This point is illustrated by Peter Johnson in his *Harvard Magazine* article describing a five-year effort to change the culture of the Bonneville Power Administration. By involving citizens in the process, innovative solutions were formulated and public acceptance more readily gained.

Evolving Environmental Ethics

Man has always had a relationship to nature. From the earliest recorded history of China, philosophers have explained how humanity relates to the "cosmic resonance theory." "Qi" (pronounced as "chee"), or essence of life, flows through everything, even inanimate objects. There is order to the universe and purpose. Humans are not distinct from nature but can use nature for human endeavors as long as coterminus subtle effects of timing and spatial positioning are in harmony. Capitalism introduced the concept of ownership, property, and alteration for human purpose. Nature is subservient to man. Air and water can be used as if they are limitless public goods. Government moderates the inefficiencies of the market system by protecting the common interest in preserving the quality of entities of air, water, and land that are in the public trust. But boundaries for intervention are quite limited and there are many instances in which government itself alters natural processes without heed.

We are now experiencing the corporate awareness that exploration and development have limits. The natural world must be better managed. Concepts like sustainable development are in the lexicon of the World Bank, the United Nations, the U.S. EPA, and multinational corporations. Sustainable development is defined as the capacity to meet the needs of the present without compromising the ability of future generations to meet their own needs. The definition is so broad that it appeals to a wide range of political and economic philosophies. As long as the definition of sustainable development is not bound to specifics of individual projects and the methodology to forecast the needs of generations yet unborn remains undeveloped, the term will remain a concept. Application of the concept to managing reduction of greenhouse gases reveals immediately the nonfeasible aspects of the generally accepted principle.

How does one generation understand the needs and aesthetic desires of future generations? It is understandable then why proponents of sustainable development believe fervently in science and technology. Science and technology, which is always advancing, becomes the cornerstone, the adjustment factor, for nonsustainable developments. Through science and technology future generations will find solutions for our problems transferred. The U.S. President's Council on Sustainable Development states that, "Advances in science and technology are beneficial to increasing understanding and the range of choices about how humanity and the environment relate." But, Albert Einstein warned us when he said "The world we have created today has created problems that cannot be solved the way we thought when we created them." More is needed than "adjusting" development projects to meet local sustainable objectives. Displaced impacts, such as greenhouse gases, nutrient runoff into marine estuaries, acid rain, and downwind ozone formation, are regional and global problems. Methodologies to make "sustainable development" a meaningful concept have not yet been devised. To postpone facing the obvious difficult choices about what type and how much development while relying on future technologies applied by future generations is foolhardy and reckless.

Under the current global market economy, commercialization of environmental technologies must have regulatory and economic drivers. Therefore, the real shift in paradigm lies in public and political persuasion that creates economic desirability and higher environmental expectations. Edgar Wollard, the President of DuPont, recognized that societal interest will be expressed in consumer preference when he said, "Corporations that think they can drag their heels indefinitely on genuine environmental problems should be advised: society won't tolerate it . . . and other companies with real sensitivity and environmental commitment will be there to supply your customers after you are gone."

The U.S. EPA Science Advisory Board (SAB) recently published the findings on future environmental problems (U.S. EPA 1995). The SAB underscores the earlier remarks by DuPont Chairman Wollard when they write that important determinants of environmental quality are the decisions and behavior of individuals, families, businesses, and communities everywhere. Environmental awareness is the key to leveraging this force. The SAB goes on to say, "A concerned, educated public, acting through responsible local, national and international institutions, will serve as effective agents for avoiding future environmental problems. . . ."

For institutions and individuals to act in environmentally responsible ways will take more than good intentions. Choices are not always straightforward, information is not readily available, and in many situations the analytic methods have not been refined. So environmentally concerned individuals and institutions do, for the most part, engage in proven yet marginally conserving activities. Then, if a cultural shift is needed, what model, philosophy, relation, or ethic do we follow?

Modern globalism as epitomized by "Earth First" movements gives a counterculture alternative. In this view nature is valued more than mankind. Preservation is necessary and essential because man has no rightful claim to exploit natural resources. This path, which strongly supports the view that excessive utilization of land and oceans must be stopped for nature's sake rather than for the long-term quality of man's survival, has drawn attention to critical issues. Among them are the loss of old growth and tropical rain forests, overharvesting of the seas, destruction of wilderness for power projects, and use of animal fur for fashion. By linking consumer consumption to environmental consequences, these organizations have made society question values. But the philosophy of "nature over man," except in specific areas (e.g., seal pup killings), cannot be expected to be mainstream. Much of the world's population is now experiencing new market economies with rising expectations for improved quality of living. It is unreasonable to expect that the desire for improved housing, better jobs, and more energy would be deferred in the interest of sustaining nature.

By what principles might individuals, institutions, corporations, and communities meld personal betterment and profit motivation to guide their decisions in an environmentally responsible manner? "Modern ecoism" has its roots in a century-old concept of "usufructuary." The nature of a usufruct is "the right to utilize and enjoy the profits and advantages of something belonging to another so long as the property is not damaged or altered in any way." Thomas Jefferson, when ambassador to France, used the term to explain his beliefs that the actions of the current generation should not indebt future generations. To Jefferson, a generation was defined by 19 years. Some of his influence is seen today in the limitation on patents and drugs. Unfortunately, concern for future generations has not guided our federal budget process.

The patterns of modern ecoism are woven into the fabric of conservation and some of this nation's earliest environmental laws on wilderness protection, endangered species, and wild rivers. Early in this century, Teddy Roosevelt said, "The nation behaves well if it treats the natural resources as assets which it must turn over to the next generation, increased and not impaired in value." Modern ecoism departs from the banking metaphor used by Roosevelt because it encompasses more than natural resources. Fundamental to modern ecoism are the writings of Jonathan Edwards. This philosopher of the New England colonies drew distinctions between a person acting as an individual and as a person acting in a relationship or connections to others. In modern parlance, it is our relationships to others that define us, not what we have done, achieved, or had bestowed upon us that makes us who we are.

Tom Chappell, an entrepreneur and businessman, talks about how Jonathan Edwards's philosophy influenced him to restructure his company. In his book *The Soul of Business,* Chappell credits Edwards for the revelation that the company, Tom's of Maine, could more fully develop its relationships, not just to customers but to employees, to the community, to suppliers, and to the environment. Essentially the "being as relationship" became the personification of the company. As it is true for man it is true for a company: relationships to others are defining.

Simply knowing the concept that everything is relationship does not guide one's actions. Those relations can be treated as objects that we dominate and control for our own gratification. In *I and Thou,* Martin Buber, a 20th century philosopher, contrasts the "I–it" relationship to the world with the "I–thou." I–thou relationships to other humans do not expect or demand a return on investment but are done for love, friendship, and respect. Tom Chappell recognized that Edwards's and Buber's philosophical tenets were corollaries in adopting them to transform his company in terms of relationships. Now Tom's of Maine offers a new model of corporate responsibility. Ingredients and packaging are evaluated in terms of their content, recycling, and even the environmental performance of suppliers. Employees are encouraged to take up to 5% of work time to volunteer; and 10% of profits sponsor a wide range of community environment projects. The company is committed to making a difference, not just a profit.

Tom's of Maine is by no means the only corporate example of modern eco-ism. Tedd Saunders, in *Bottom Line of Black is Green,* describes the environmental initiatives of his family's hotels and those of many other companies. Recycling, energy conservation, redesigned packaging, efficient lighting, specifying environmental attributes for supplies (cleaners, paints, etc.) are often-cited examples. Few companies extend product stewardship to ensure compliance of their secondary manufacturers with environmental and occupational health and safety requirements.

Not many companies, particularly not larger corporations, have broken so radically from traditional structure and behavior as Tom's of Maine and Ben & Jerry's. Ben Cohen and Jerry Greenfield started an ice cream company in Waterbury, Vermont, that was dedicated to using natural ingredients, making a profit, and promoting social good. In less than 20 years they were distributing nationally, yet they have adhered to their principles of profit sharing, respecting employees, selecting materials with an environmental perspective, and sponsoring civic activities. For the practices of these companies to become less the exception and more the rule, we need new economic models to incorporate how community goodwill, employee motivation, and careful material selection can increase productivity, preserve resources (environment), satisfy investors, and return a fair profit.

The real challenge is adapting the principles that guide these companies in such a way to guide our communities and other institutions. The World Health Organization's (WHO) Healthy Cities Program brings together disparate sectors of city management, commerce, and the public to formulate a process to identify goals and means toward healthier urban living. But we will need more public and private organization to reappraise their purpose and rethink their influence. Total quality management should mean more than satisfying customers or reducing product defects. For cities to enhance the quality of life while reducing the ecological burden, its member institutions must integrate these goals into their organizational structure and function. Through collective choices, society's members must encourage and reward ecologically responsible behavior.

Summary

What have we accomplished with cities? Cities have served many functions over time: security, authority, and commerce, among others. For about

10,000 years, cities as a concept of social and commercial organization have had strategic advantages, independent of political-monetary models. Cities have prospered because of trade, transportation, and employment. Technological innovations, such as elevators, electricity, and centralized water treatment, have helped to sustain urbanized development. Public and private investments promote urban vitality. The examples are abundant: modernized airports from Atlanta to Denver, roads and bridges, and the citification of the Virginia and Maryland suburbs encouraged by the Washington Metro.

There have been massive changes in the underlying fabric of cities. Early in the next millennium half the world's population will live in urban areas. In 1950 there were only 12 cities with a population of more than 4 million. Soon there will be more than 65 densely populated urban areas around the world. In reality, the city function has been reversed to where cities may concentrate capital wealth but house most of the poor. Already, we see that in excess of 50% of the populations in cities like Calcutta, São Paulo, and Ibadan in Nigeria live in slums on the fringes. Even in the United States, the blight and poverty of decaying public housing are obvious reminders that the financial assets of cities are differentially held by those not living in the cities. Cities are not protected by ramparts but surrounded by commuter beltways. So it should not be surprising that today's cities are polluted and less safe.

Yet, cities offer a solution. Economical and conserving use of land, materials, and energy could reduce the per capita consumption rate of air and water while further reducing the waste. The World Health Organization Healthy Cities Program, the new European Community working on the "Ecological City," and examples of enlightened organization or urban development in Toronto, Canada; Chattanooga, Tennessee; and Curatiba, Brazil, offer models that embody "modern ecoism." Modern ecoism exists where resource reduction, pollution prevention, product stewardship, and recycling are promoted and when responsible institutions are in partnership with nature. The concept is more than "sustainable development." Political and economic leaders have quickly embraced the concept of sustainable development to guide investment. However, there is neither an agreement on how to assess the environmental implications of development nor a commonly accepted set of indices to measure progress. Underlying the term "sustainable development" is the implicit faith that technology will be available to solve problems displaced to the future.

It is clear that technology is necessary to solve many of the environmental, housing, energy, and transportation problems of cities. Just as automobiles, high-rises, and subways transformed cities over the 20th century, technology of the 21st century will continue to redefine urban life. New technology is asked to solve social, health, and environmental problems. For mega-cities to be healthful for their inhabitants, we will need fewer vehicle miles traveled in automobiles, not simply cleaner emissions. We will need less air conditioning for buildings, more reflective architectural coatings, reduced packaging, and reformulated products, among many new and innovative approaches. Corporations, institutions, and individuals must redefine themselves in the contexts of numerous interrelated associations. Individuals and institutions working within the constraints of natural systems will be the defining difference if the future is to be sustainable.

Acknowledgments

Professor Robert Geddes (New York University) and Dean Peter Rowe (Harvard University) gave us the opportunity to step back from our academic responsibilities to reflect on the environmental challenges of urban settlements. Solutions to many of our ecological problems must be formulated through the multisector dynamic of urban communities. At the same time, we are concerned that societies singularly dedicated to growth may fail to incorporate environmental ethics into planning. Our prospective academic institutions must be managed in environmentally responsible ways and promote a mature ecological consciousness throughout our curricula.

We also thank Dr. Haluk Özkaynak and Ms. Joan Arnold for their contributions to this chapter.

References

ATS (American Thoracic Society) (1990). Environmental controls and lung disease. *Am. Rev. Respir. Dis.* 142:915.

Beaton, S.P., Bishop, G.A., Zhang, Y., Ashbaugh, L.L., Lawson, D.R., and Stedman, D.H. (1995). On-road vehicle emissions: Regulations, costs, and benefits. *Science* 268:945–1100.

Burge, S., Hedge, A., Wilson, S., Bass, J.H., and Robertson, A. (1987). Sick building syndrome: A study of 4373 workers. *Ann. Occup. Hyg.* 31:493–504.

Burnett, R.T., Dales, R.E., Raizenne, M.E., Krewski, D., Summers, P.W., Roberts, G.R., Young, M.R., Dann, T., and Brooke, J. (1993). Effects of low ambient levels of ozone and sulfates on the frequency of respiratory admissions to Ontario hospitals. *Environ. Res.* 65:172–194.

CIAQ (Committee on Indoor Air Quality) (1987). *Policies and Procedures for Control of Indoor Air Quality in Existing Buildings.* Washington, DC: National Academy Press.

Cone, J.E., and Hodgson, M.J. (eds.) (1989). Problem buildings: Building-associated illness and the sick building syndrome. *Occup. Med.* 4(4):575–797.

Dockery, D.W., Schwartz, J., and Spengler, J.D. (1992). Air pollution and daily mortality: Associations with particulates and acid aerosols. *Environ. Res.* 59:362–373.

Dockery, D.W., Pope, C.A., Xiping, X., Spengler, J.D., Ware, J.H., Fay, M.E., Ferris, B.G., and Speizer, F.E. (1993). An association between air pollution and mortality in six U.S. cities. *N. Engl. J. Med.* 329:1753–1759.

Duplaix, N. (1990). South Florida water: Paying the price. *National Geographic* 178(1):89–113.

Fairley, D. (1990). The relationship of daily mortality to suspended particulates in Santa Clara County, 1980–1986. *Environ. Health Perspect.* 89:159–168.

Finnegan, M.J., Pickering, C.A.C., and Burge, P.S. (1984). The sick building syndrome: Prevalence studies. *Br. Med. J.* 289:1573–1575.

Ford, T.E. (1993). The microbial ecology of water distribution and outfall systems. In Ford, T.E. (ed.), *Aquatic Microbiology—An Ecological Approach.* Boston: Blackwell, pp. 455–482.

Gammage, R.B., and Kaye, S.V. (eds.) (1985). *Indoor Air and Human Health.* Chelsea, MI: Lewis Publishers.

Gleick, P.H. (ed.) (1993). *Water in Crisis.* New York: Oxford University Press, p. 473.

Gyntelberg, F., Suadicani, P., Nielsen, J.W., Skov, P., Valbjørn, O., Nielsen, P.A., Schneider, T., Jorgensen, O., Wolkoff, P., Wilkins, C.K., Gravesen, S., and Norn, S. (1994). Dust and the sick-building syndrome. *Indoor Air* 4:223–238.

Hodgson, M. (1989). Clinical diagnosis and management of building related illness and the sick building syndrome. *Occup. Med.* 4:593–606.

Hollowell, C.D., and Miksch, R.R. (1981). Sources and concentrations of organic compounds in indoor air environments. *Bull. NY Acad. Med.* 57:962.

Holquin, A.H., Buffler, P.A., and Contant, C.F. (1985). The effects of ozone on asthmatics in the Houston area. In Lee, S.D. (ed.) *Evaluation of the Scientific Basis for Ozone/Oxidant Standards.* Pittsburgh: Air Pollution Control Association, pp. 150–261.

Johnson, P.T. (1993). How I turned a critical public into useful consultants. *Harvard Business Review,* Jan.–Feb. 1993, pp. 55–56.

Kaminiski, J.C., MacKenzie, W.R., Addiss, D.G., and Davis, J.P. (1994). Cryptosporidium and the Public Water Supply (correspondence). *N. Engl. J. Med.* 331:1529–1530.

Kinney, P.L., and Özkaynak, H. (1991). Associations of daily mortality and air pollution in Los Angeles County. *Environ. Res.* 54:99–120.

Klein, P.D., Graham, D.Y., Gaillour, A., Opekun, A.R., and Smith, E.O. (1991).

Water source as risk factor for *Helicobacter pylori* infection in Peruvian children. *Lancet* 337:1503–1506.

Kramer, M.H.J., and Ford, T.E. (1994). Legionellosis: Ecological factors of an environmentally 'new disease.' *Zbl. Hyg.* 195:470–482.

Kreiss, K. (1989). The epidemiology of building-related complaints and illness. *Occup. Med.* 4:575.

Lebret, E., van der Wiel, H.J., Bos, H.P., Noij, D., and Boleij, J.S.M. (1986). Volatile organics in Dutch homes. *Environ. Int.* 12:323–332.

MacKenzie, W.R., Hoxie, N.J., Proctor, M.E., et al. (1994). A massive outbreak in Milwaukee of cryptosporidium infection transmitted through the public water supply. *N. Engl. J. Med.* 331:161–167.

McDonnell, W.F., Dehrl, H.R., Abdul-Salaam, S., Ives, P.J., Folinsbee, L.J., Devlin, R.B., O'Neil, J.J., and Horstman, D.H. (1991). Respiratory response of humans exposed to low levels of ozone for 6.6 hours. *Arch. Environ. Health* 46:145–150.

Molhave, L. (1985). Volatile organic compounds as indoor air pollutants. *In* Gammage, R.B., and Kaye, S.V. (eds.), *Indoor Air and Human Health.* Chelsea, MI: Lewis Publishers, pp. 403–414.

Molhave, L. (1987). The sick buildings—A subpopulation among the problem buildings? *In* Seifert, B., Esorn, H., Fischer, M., et al. (eds.), *Indoor Air '87, Proceedings of the 4th International Conference on Indoor Air Quality and Climate* Berlin: Institute for Water, Soil, and Air Hygiene, Vol. 2, pp. 469–473.

Office of Technology Assessment (1985). *Acid Rain and Transported Air Pollutants: Implications for Public Policy.* New York: UNIPUB, published in cooperation with the Office of Technology Assessment, Congress of the U.S., Washington, D.C., Library of Congress Catalog Card Number 84-52370.

Özkaynak, H. (1993). Review of recent epidemiological data on health effects of particles, ozone and nitrogen dioxide. Paper presented at the Conference on Clean Air Challenges in a Changing South Africa, Dikhololo, South Africa, November 11–12, 1993.

Özkaynak, H., and Kinney, P.L. (1995). Associations of daily mortality and air pollution in New York City. Manuscript in preparation.

Özkaynak, H., Xue, J., Severance, P., Burnett, R., and Raizenne, M. (1993). Associations between daily mortality, ozone and particulate air pollution in Toronto, Canada. Paper presented at the colloquium on "Particulate Air Pollution and Human Mortality and Morbidity." Irvine, CA, January 24–25, 1993.

Özkaynak, H., Kinney, P.L., and Burbank, B. (1990). Recent epidemiological findings on morbidity and mortality effects of ozone. Paper presented at the 83rd Annual Meeting & Exhibition of Air & Waste Management Association. Pittsburgh, PA, June 24–29, 1990.

Pope, C.A. III, Schwartz, J., and Ransom, M.R. (1992). Daily mortality and PM_{10} pollution in Utah Valley. *Arch. Environ. Health* 47:211–217.

Pope, C.A. III, Thun, M.J., Namboodiri, M.M., Dockery, D.W., Evans, J.S., Speizer, F.E., and Heath, C.W., Jr. (1995). Particulates air pollution as a predictor of mortality in a prospective study of the U.S. adults. *Am. J. Respir. Crit. Care Med.* 151:669–674.

Quinlan, P., Macher, P.M., Alevantis, L.E., and Cone, J.E. (1989). Protocol for the comprehensive evaluation of building-associated illness. *Occup. Med.* 4:771–797.

Raizenne, M.E., and Spengler, J.D. (1989). Dosimetric model of acute health effects of ozone and acid aerosols in children. *In* Schneider, T., et al. (eds.), *Atmospheric Ozone Research and its Policy Implications.* Amsterdam: Elsevier Science Publishers, pp. 319–329.

Saunders, T., and McGovern, L. (1993). *The Bottom Line of Green is Black.* New York: HarperCollins Publishers.

Schwartz, J. (1991). Particulate air pollution and daily mortality in Detroit. *Environ. Res.* 56:204–213.

Schwartz, J. (1993). Air pollution and daily mortality in Birmingham, AL. *Am. J. Epidemiol.* 137:1136–1147.

Schwartz, J., and Dockery, D.W. (1992a). Increased mortality in Philadelphia associated with daily air pollution concentrations. *Am. Rev. Respir. Dis.* 145:600–604.

Schwartz, J., and Dockery, D.W. (1992b). Particulate air pollution and daily mortality in Steubenville, Ohio. *Am. J. Epidemiol.* 135:12–19.

Spengler, J.D., Brauer, M., and Koutrakis, P. (1990). Acid air and health. *Environ. Sci. Technol.* 24:946–956.

Spengler, J.D., Hollowell, C., Moschandreas, D., and Fanger, O. (eds.). (1982). Indoor air pollution (special issue). *Environ. Int.* 8:3–351.

Thurston, G.D., Ito, K., Kinney, P.L., and Lippmann, M. (1992). A multi-year study of air pollution and respiratory hospital admissions in three New York state metropolitan area: Results for 1988 and 1989 summers. *J. Expo. Anal. Dis. Environ. Epidemiol.* 2:429–450.

Thurston, G.D., Ito, K., and Lippman, M. (1993). The role of particulate mass vs. acidity in the sulfate-respiratory hospital admissions associations. Paper presented at the 86th Annual Meeting & Exhibition of the Air & Waste Management Association. Denver, CO, June 13–18, 1993.

U.S. EPA (1994). *National Air Quality and Emission Trend Report.* U.S. Environmental Protection Agency, Office of Air Quality Planning and Standards, Research Triangle Park, NC 27711, EPA 454/RO94-026, October 1994.

U.S. EPA (1995). *Beyond the Horizon: Using Foresight to Protect the Environmental Future.* U.S. EPA Science Advisory Board, Environmental Futures Committee, January 1995.

Wapner, K. (1993). A tale of calves, Catskills and *E. coli*. *The Amicus Journal* 5(3):29–30.

Whittemore, A.S., and Korn, E.L. (1980). Asthma and air pollution in the Los Angeles area. *Am. J. Public Health* 70:687–696.

WHO (World Health Organization) (1982). *Indoor Air Pollutants Exposure and Health Effects Assessment.* World Health Organization, Geneva, EURO Reports and Studies 78, Working Group Report.

Zwingle, E. (1993). Wellspring of the high plains. *National Geographic* 183(3):80–109.

Case Studies

Los Angeles
and Its Region

At the end of the 20th century, Los Angeles is the "shock city" of our time, like Manchester, England, in the 19th century, and New York in the early 20th century. Moreover, it is now seen as "the first *American* city," the first to remove itself from the European models of growth and form.

In his case study, Richard Weinstein (an architect and urban designer) approaches Los Angeles from the perspective of American cultural studies. He weaves together insights from history, poetry, and social criticism to arrive at the conclusion that "the structure of the built environment as it exists in Los Angeles now represents a paradigm for growth that already houses more than half of the (U.S.) population and is, with variations, the pattern of growth for most new settlements in the developed world."

What is the Los Angeles paradigm? It is an extended, open, unbounded matrix laced with linear corridors, from boulevard to strips, and overlaid by freeways. Its key words are: fragmented, incomplete, ad hoc, uncentered. As urban form, it stands in sharp contrast to the dense grid of Manhattan, and to the multi-centered structure of post-war Toronto.

Concerning the Los Angeles environment, it is argued that the open extended matrix, with all its in-between spaces, is more adaptable to environmental health factors than denser, more continuous urban structures. There is more green, in between.

But, with respect to social equity, the outcome of the Los Angeles urban form may be negative. The openness of its matrix easily supports ethnic colonies and may even promote their social segregation, isolation, and fragmentation.

Does Los Angeles demonstrate the ideal spatial structure for new economic patterns to emerge, "a mulch for new jobs"? If the goal is to balance the economy, the environment, and social equity, is the open, extended matrix the inevitable urban form of a free, democratic society?

Los Angeles: The First American City

Richard Weinstein

Los Angeles is the first consequential American city to separate itself decisively from European models and to reveal the impulse to privatization imbedded in the origins of the American Revolution. Some have emphasized the operation of economic factors in the development of Los Angeles, but these need to be understood.in relation to cultural and ideological forces of singular power and resilience. While these forces influenced the economic marketplace, they cannot be explained as arising exclusively from its operation.

In order to understand Los Angeles and the many places like it, certain recurring themes in American culture need to be examined—themes that arise from attitudes toward nature and society and the city as they were affected by the experience of settling a new continent; the transformation of that experience by science and industrial change; and by the optimistic linkage of both to our national destiny, to the conquest of western space, and to the destruction of native populations. These experiences and their representation in art, literature, and thought provide the context of values that guide our choices as a people. The operation of the marketplace is an indicator of these deeper inclinations as they interact with the uncertainties of the modern condition. But it also is itself formative of their ultimately American expressions in the political and institutional arrangements we have made, in new sensibilities that alter our perceptions, and in the environment we have built (which is their reflection) and reaches a culmination in the urban pattern of Los Angeles.

The hope that the new world inspired in the European mind was premised in part on the dream of Arcadia, but from the beginning the idea of the

United States was also bound up with the idea of economic self-sufficiency, improvisation, tinkering, ingenuity, the empirical and the practical, within the abundant context of a natural bounty. Thus began the American drama opposing the hope for material progress to the dangerous mystery of nature.

In Los Angeles, however debased, however partial in its expression, however compromised has been the sublime principle of desert, mountain, and sea, these great cultural themes have found their most complete expression.

> The houses and the automobiles are equal figments of a great dream, the dream of the urban homestead, the dream of a good life outside the squalor of the European type of city, and thus a dream that runs back not only into the Victorian railway suburbs of earlier cities, but also to the country-house culture of the fathers of the U.S. Constitution, or the whig squirearchs whose spiritual heirs they sometimes were, and beyond them to the "villegiatura" of Palladio's patrons, of the Medicis' "Poggio a Caiano." Los Angeles cradles and embodies the most potent current version of the great bourgeois vision of the good life in a tamed countryside. . . .
>
> —Reyner Banham

Natural Crimes

The early citizens of the United States occupied a neutral, middle ground between a removal from European influence, and the sense of a violent frontier to the west where Native Americans resisted the encroachment of a more powerful civilization. The protection of private rights afforded by the Constitution was enhanced in the agricultural countryside bordering the frontier by the reality and dangers of spatial isolation. Whatever was other became a threat. The destruction of native populations was rationalized on the basis of survival, on the basis of conversion to the faith, and on the basis of the "superior" message of Western civilization. Though the government's record of broken treaties was dismal, it nevertheless showed recognition of certain entitlement that the native populations had. This was perhaps influenced by ideas about noble savage, closeness to nature, and even the evidence of native genius.

What is relevant, however, is the strategy of sequestering the other within defined spatial borders (the reservations), and the use of violent action to achieve these ends. In the process, violence became a justified instrument of segregation and conquest, and racial difference became an acceptable cause for such action when it served the collective interest of the pioneers. As a result, fundamental contradictions, if not crimes, were built into the formative experience of the nation that proclaimed the equality of all men and their right to the pursuit of happiness. These means corrupted the moral underpinning of democratic institutions that sought a system of government that would resolve disputes before violent means became necessary. These violent means that were applied to native populations were also applied to nature, which was savaged and consumed in the movement west.

Racism and violence in American culture, and its expression in spatial terms, was both rationalized by dangerous encounters on the frontier and supported by the attitudes and practices of slavery in the South—it was reinforced by private entitlement that gave emphasis to the idea of the other, and haunted by the influence of nature as simultaneously a source of redemptive knowledge and the carrier of savage threats to survival.

One consequence of these attitudes was the early separation of white immigrant populations in Los Angeles from the existing Hispanic settlements. Over time this led to the introduction of single-use zoning not only to isolate culture enclaves but to separate residential areas from noxious manufacturing zones and crowding that had polluted older cities.

The earlier history of Los Angeles is fouled by a series of violent racial incidents against Chinese and Hispanic populations that culminated in the century's two most serious civil disturbances, the Watts and Los Angeles riots.

Culture as Empiricism and Machine

The distrust of urban civilization, joined with the sense of boundless space, movement, and opportunity, was strengthened as industry changed the character of the great urban centers. Pollution, crime, immigration, noise, traffic, and poverty were increasingly seen as threats to the good life and in fundamental opposition to the Jeffersonian strain in the American character. These sentiments were given new form by Thoreau and Emerson, though with a transcendental, romantic coloring. Accelerated by the railroads, the suburbs

> . . . express a complex and compelling vision of the modern family freed from the corruption of the city, restored to harmony with nature, endowed with wealth and independence, yet protected by a close-knit, stable community.

As Lewis Mumford also said in *The Culture of Cities,* "The suburbs are a collective effort to live a private life."

By the mid-1850s, urban areas were feeling the impact of industrialization, and Emerson had begun to state his case against scientific rationality and its industrial consequences. In *Nature,* published in 1836, he argues that experimental science is necessarily preoccupied with function and process, and that "a dream may let us deeper into the secrets of nature than a hundred concerted experiments." Emerson sensed a turning point in American values when he further criticized practical intelligence as being morally neutral, and potentially dangerous. He prescribed immersion in the natural landscape as spiritual therapy. George Orwell would later observe, "So long as a machine is *there,* one is under an obligation to use it"; while Siegfried Gideon, certain of progress, stated, "If possible, then necessary," and Mulholland (of the water he brought to LA from the desert), "There it is, take it."

This ideology of industrialization was thus premised and rationalized, as Leo Marx has shown, on the notion of nature as a divine machine and was identified with the notion of progress itself. The intervention of machines to do the labor of humans became associated with the American myth of unlimited progress and hope.

The image of suburban America in the early part of the 20th century domesticates some of these themes. It was Frederick Law Olmsted who advocated the continuity of suburban front lawns as a means of expressing amplitude and democratic communal solidarity. The American obsession with front lawns reveals a deeper ideological inclination. The lawn also represents a subjugation of nature to the rule of civilization. It is an abstraction of the presence of nature, like the whiteness of Moby Dick; it is nature known and therefore tamed. As Michael Pollan has observed, the democracy of the suburban lawn is simultaneously benign, excessive, and obsessive in the sense that it imposes a sameness irrespective of geographic difference and the particularity of ecological place. At the same time the lawn is pleasing, ordinary, democratic, and allows each citizen a symbolic share in a domesticated ritual of subjugation and aggrandizement. The lawn is a middle-class embodiment of the American conflict between the value of nature as a principle and its management as a means toward material progress. Whitman's poetry earlier expressed these contradictions, with more explicit expansionist overtones. His was a kind of romantic poetry of the democratic collective that was self-justifying and gave a moral gloss to those who in celebrating themselves were also identifying with the spirit of patriotic conquest and manifest destiny.

Los Angeles emerges as the dominant expression of these contradictory impulses and values that need to be understood as they interact with other powerful forces, the natural landscape and climate, economic growth, the character of migration, the national impulse toward suburbanization, the railroad, and later the automobile.

> I sing of myself.
> —Walt Whitman

To American attitudes toward nature and industrialization, the linkage between the nuclear family and the suburban impulse, and the practical optimism associated with an expanded frontier, must be added a changing view of individual fulfillment. Once again it is Emerson who gave concentrated expression to the more general sentiment when he declared that wealth was less a measure of achievement than a means to "the legitimate comforts of [a well-rounded] life." The significance of this attitude lies in what it tells us about the waning of the agrarian myth and the Protestant ethic. Work is no longer conceived as possessing inherent, if not religiously justified, value; rather it is perceived as standing in relation to a holistic notion of the good life, centered on individual rather than collective experience—emphasizing the transcendental and later to be romantic impulse rather than traditional Protestant virtue.

The rise of evangelical Christianity in various forms may be seen as a counter revolutionary and conservative move to protect religious values threatened both by the Industrial Revolution and by the privatization of religious experience proposed by Emerson, Thoreau, and Whitman.

> I make my circumstances . . . I—this thought which is called I—is the mold into which the word is poured like melted wax. . . . You call it the power of circumstance, but it is the power of me.
> —Ralph Waldo Emerson

In the last half of the 19th century, significant changes had occurred in the American idea of success. The shift was away from the work ethic and toward mental self-determination. Richard Weiss summarizes:

> The success myth's popularity was, in large measure, due to the moral certainty it offered in a period of profound dislocation and confusion. The inequities produced by industrialization did not merely outrage the sense of justice; they threatened to shatter an habitual way of viewing the world and interpreting experience. Purveyors of the protestant ethic sensed this threat and responded with assertions of traditional morality. Social, economic, and intellectual changes, however, challenged more than ideal conceptions of behav-

ior; these changes fostered a deterministic view of man which ran counter to the world view implicit in success mythology. The cult of mind and mind-power was a response to this deeper challenge. Proponents of the mentalist success cult were self-conscious defenders of an idealistic view of man and the cosmos. Their idealism struck a responsive chord because it made possible the continued belief in the individual's power to mold his own life in a society where men seemed increasingly subject to forces beyond their control. The idea which links the two success mythologies in their common definition of the successful life is one which is self-willed, self-directed, and self-controlled. Preserving this belief in the power of self-determination as a possibility for all men was the chief factor operating in the change from the old to the new success tradition.

In the early 1900s, William James emphasized the essential unity of physical and mental action and pointed to the efficacy of the brain in helping to overcome the actual, physical difficulties of life. In this he showed himself to be in the tradition of Emerson, and related to the "New Thought" that included the contemporary mentalist religion of Christian Science. James argued that belief can condition reality, ". . . *where faith in a fact can help create the fact.*" Such sentiments can be found pervasively in the popular literature of the time, which emphasizes fulfillment and self-realization, time for leisure, the avoidance of conflict, and the generally positive view of life that has come to be identified with Southern California.

Those who found comfort and motivation in these ideas, which James likened to a pervasive religious awakening, were drawn to Southern California, where they were persuaded that climate and life-style would support their inclination. Here they could, like Emerson, ignore "experience whenever it was in harsh or ugly conflict with (their) optimism." George Santayana, then at Harvard with James and Josiah Royce, remarked that these future citizens of Southern California, were the ". . . sentimentalists, mystics, spiritualists, wizards, cranks, quacks, and impostors . . . those groping, nervous, half-educated, spiritually disinherited, passionately hungry, individuals of which America is full." They were not only produced by the place, or by the character of economic forces, they also constructed the place in the image of their inclinations.

By the turn of the century these attitudinal changes had ripened in the affluent, small-town Middle West—as Robert Fogelson notes, "Holding traditional sentiments about the moral superiority of the countryside they were increasingly reluctant to be bound to rural drudgery"—and it was to this population that the boosters of Southern California turned their avid attention with booming success in the early years of the century. Los Angeles was described as "The Middle West brought to a flash point." The village was the settlement pattern that most appealed to those who considered moving to Southern California; ". . . it is our departure from these 'village ideals,' said one new settler, the simple, comely life of our fathers, that has nurtured the blight of demoralizing metropolitanism, a curse alike to old and young. . . ." These provincial ideals also placed a value on social harmony, the absence of conflict, and hence the exclusion of nonconforming racial groups, in order to allay the anxieties associated with the move west. The promoters of Southern California real estate promised at the same time the recovery of an idealized life of the village in a rural setting, and the opportunity for personal fulfillment.

At the beginning of the century, the Red Cars of Huntington provided a decentralized mass transit network of trolleys that facilitated the pattern of linked suburban village settlements dispersed over the landscape that irreversibly established the fundamental pattern of Los Angeles's regional growth. This pattern, reinforced by land values and accessibility, responded to the persistent yearning in the American character for a redemptive contact with nature represented by the West, an escape from the failures of the industrial metropolis, the changes in the notion of the good life, family, and personal destiny.

That this paradigmatic post-modern urban form should have found its first and still most comprehensive expression in Los Angeles is in part the result of the dispersed spatial infrastructure of the first significant immigrations that enabled, and even encouraged, the transformations that have occurred since the 1960s.

The Extended City

The prevailing extended city is now characterized by a medium-density housing tissue of subdivisions, laced with commercial strips including small industrial spaces, and periodically marked by centers of varying size that consist of a shopping mall with a cineplex, a cluster of commercial buildings, a health care facility. At intervals, zones of industrial space form the hinterland behind the commercial arteries. This pattern occurs with variations at more or less regular intervals governed by the appetites of the marketplace in which each commercial or retail use depends for its success on access to a certain residential population. Because much of the U.S. population now lives in the extended city, it is possible to describe its characteristics as a particular kind of market where predictable typologies regularly occur in response to subsets of population.

Three characteristics may serve to describe this built environment. The *matrix* is the prevailing latticework of intersecting grids in which a variety of uses are distributed. This matrix is laced by *linear developments* of greater commercial density from boulevards down to strips. Density is also clustered at *nodes* or activity centers. These repetitive patterns are also reflected in the fragmented institutional and political structure of the region that is composed of over 50 municipalities, of county governments, and of a variety of wealthy, autonomous, single-purpose, air quality, transportation, water, waste management, and redevelopment agencies. Many citizens are most directly affected by homeowners' associations in which voting rights are proportional to the value of the owner's property. At the periphery of the extended city, development may occur in unincorporated territory without adequate political representation. In addition, the rapid growth of the extended city corresponds with the accelerated entry of women into the work force in the 1970s, and the consequent proliferation of automobile ownership.

Among the causes of these social transformations were new economic pressures and the destabilizing uncertainties associated with rapid change, but also the burdens associated with individual choice, unsupported by a prevailing system of public values. "The enchantment of our souls by myth, philosophy, and revelation, has been replaced by more immediate meaning—the building of free and equal men by the overcoming of chance." One response to the emerging role of uncertainty may be themed attractions like Disneyland.

> History has no dominion over such a world. Instead time was contingent and malleable. Without a past firmly situated in relation to the future, there were no beginnings or endings, no death.
> —Karal Ann Marling

The interchangeability, predictability, and ordinariness of this urban landscape also offers comfort and security to a mobile population, anxiety ridden in the pursuit of profit, pleasure, individual self-definition, and the control of chance. Yet, the ordinary, common, and conforming still contribute to this anxiety by a tense relation to the singular, individual, and privatized.

The complexity and fragmentation of governance arrangements, and the multiple regulatory maze that is precipitated by their operation, make political accountability almost impossible. The physical and spatial structure of the region is therefore inseparably related to the institutional and political arrangements that constitute its governance. The primary image of the city is of an extended repetitive fabric, bounded by the sea or mountain edge and overlaid with a discontinuous, contrapuntal net of freeways, with periodic concentrations of high-rise developments that are conceptually mapped during high-speed travel. The physical characteristics of the place are the objective correlative for its privatized, insular, fragmented, institutional structure, bound to some rule of reason, as by the freeways, through the establishment of imperial bureaucracies. The absence of integrated hierarchical order in either the built or institutional environment is in some sense the complete expression of the kind of democracy that accompanies an apotheosis of privatization where the multiplicity of competing parts leads to a uniform texture of alienated political activity. John Cage, who lived in Los Angeles, developed a musical metaphor which embodies the same characteristics. He described his compositions as, ". . . setting a process going which has no necessary beginning, no middle, no end, and no sections."

Fragmenting discontinuities operated on both the new development and infill between existing (but already dispersed) communities that preceded the automobile, becoming the nonhierarchical, flexible, extended matrix that characterizes Los Angeles. The spatial porosity of the system, its void/positive character, together with the blockages represented by parking structures, and the emptiness of parking lots and huge wholesale warehouses, effectively preclude the hierarchical, linear, narrative ordering of traditional urban space with its organized public realm that depend either on consensual or authoritarian politics, and the traditionally clear separation of public and private space.

In the European city, the public realm is usually apprehended as an open space within a communal solid; our impression of such cities is that they are mass-positive residuals of the feudal city, out of which were carved the piazzas and boulevards. Were it possible to oppose the deep impulse toward democratic privatization, the urban design strategies to create a similar postmodern public realm are not obvious. In Los Angeles, such realms are natural—the beach, the mountains, the desert. But these are not civic realms, they are essentially private experiences of nature.

To them must be added the theme park that appeals to our lost sense of community.

> In a pluralistic society, where experiences of church, school, and ethnicity were not universally shared, Disney motifs constituted a common culture, a kind of civil religion of happy endings, worry free consumption, technological optimism, and nostalgia for the good old days.

Disneyland, observed Charles Moore ". . . is keyed to the kind of participation without embarrassment . . . we crave."

Themed developments are increasingly a part of Southern California life and real estate strategies and are linked to retail, hotel, and restaurant planning.

The yearning for the fulfillment of this ideal can be sensed underneath the distraught conditions of contemporary Los Angeles, in the arrangements of its built form in relation to nature, in the managed innocence of its themed cultural productions. However, the sense of tragic limits, arising from the sediment of history out of which the structure of older cities are made, is crucially absent here, where the individual pursuit of paradise, the will "to triumph by earthly happiness," has become the shaping influence.

Repetitive patterns and typologies, however they respond to valid psychic needs that underlie and motivate the behavior of the market, also address issues of efficient mass production and convenience for the majority population.

> The strip is trying to tell us something about ourselves: namely that most Americans prefer convenience, are determined to simplify as much of the mechanical service and distribution sides of life as possible, and are willing to subsidize any informal geographic setting that helps.
>
> —J.B. Jackson

These strategies combine to undermine the authenticity of unique places, in favor of uniformity of treatment—in fact, ". . . the absence of place permits the attainment of greater levels of spatial (economic) efficiency." Or put differently by J.B. Jackson:

> What survived of that earlier vernacular culture was its . . . adaptability, its preference for the transitory, the ephemeral. Our vernacular landscape has unparalleled vitality and diversity, but it . . . (is detached) from formal space . . . (it is indifferent) to history . . . essentially utilitarian, conscienceless (in its) use of the environment.

The strip and its perfection in the shopping mall, as well as the huge block-busting wholesale outlets, are a logical solution to the problem of optimizing the acquisition of goods and services. The persistence of the form everywhere offers familiar access to the newcomer and minimizes adjustment (and presumed discomfort) to a new setting.

Much has been made of the homogeneity of subdivision design; despite the stylistic surface distinctions between New England or Spanish themes, houses and their internal arrangement are essentially the same from place to place. This has been attributed by Garreau to the national mobility of the buyers, who move on an average of every six years to pursue new job opportunities—perhaps four or five moves in a working life. Homes are treated as investments, and by avoiding eccentricities, a more uniform (and hence liquid) market is created, which appeals to a broader spectrum of buyers. The anxiety associated with job mobility and the uprooting of the family from place to place may also account in part for the value attached to the predictability (interchangeability) of environments and their signal features, such as gated entrances.

New urban settlements, exemplified by Los Angeles, are characterized by families in which both parents work, in which shopping and business destinations are distributed throughout a medium-density matrix, and in which employment destinations change with job mobility. These shifting, multiple targets, and the consequent low rail ridership, effectively preclude fixed rail as a transit strategy, and make a mockery of any jobs/housing balance. The extended city suggests other modes of transit (e.g., the smart shuttle, which is demand-activated and satellite- and computer-controlled).

The spatial dispersion of Los Angeles is also inseparably related to its economic vigor and has produced the strongest and most diversified regional economy in the country. This is a contract-based economy with 75% of the businesses employing fewer than ten workers. These businesses form and disperse with changes in international markets, available real estate, and patterns of immigration. The spatial porosity of the built environment facilitates the formation of economic "sticky clusters," where the subcontractors needed to serve an emerging industry (e.g., medical instruments) can assemble. The continued spread of extended cities may be linked to the provision of affordable real estate as one condition of innovation and economic expansion.

The Experience of the Extended City

Conceive of a space that is filled with moving.
—Gertrude Stein (In response to the question, "What is America?")

The uncertainty, the dissolving, and chance conditions of contemporary life are reflected in the ad hoc texture of the Los Angeles urban landscape; it is the lack of hierarchical organization at the scale of neighborhoods that permits this impression to flourish. Vacant lots, parking lots, irrational leftover spaces that are the residual of freeway construction, impermeable parking

structures, and the repetitive patterns that destroy the possibility of an as-
cending order promote the sense of porosity, flux, and impermanence. Further, the temporary and flimsy character of much construction contributes to
the sense of instability and impermanence that, in the early state of decay,
forms a kind of inexpensive mulch in which the small industrial entrepreneurs who form the base of the region's manufacturing economy appear to
flourish.

The city is experienced as a passage through space, with constraints established by speed and motion, rather than the static condition of solids, of
buildings that define the pedestrian experience of traditional cities. The resulting detachment further privatizes experience, devalues the public realm,
and, by force of the time spent in travel, contributes to isolation. Increasingly,
social interaction is structured not by shared experience but by the comparison of solitary encounters with media events—even when the event is riot
or war. Our experience of the physical structure of Los Angeles, its nonhierarchical, unordered presence, and our compartmentalized, multileveled,
multiscaled, and fragmented impression of it, seems to be the world Marx described as melting into air.

Yet there is a subtext of concern for the development and discovery of the
self as a moral exercise that touches on the idea of a moral commonwealth, a
concern for the natural environment, an immediate pleasure in nature that
has contributed to an open, informal, and inclusive life-style, increasingly influenced by Asian culture, and the development of a regional architecture inspired by the work of Frank Gehry that suggests the existence of deeper
forces at work.

In assembling what is deficient and dangerous in the extended city, it is
also important to point out opportunities for change and adaptability that
also inhere in the way its physical frame is constructed. First, the extended
city lends itself to change because so much of it is open space. Second, because the quality of much construction is ersatz, in part due to the permis-
siveness of climate, it is relatively easy to renew and change. Third, because
density is dispersed, it is possible to provide for growth in almost unnotice-
able increments if it were to be uniformly distributed. The capacity to absorb
growth also implies the flexibility to allow for selective concentrations of
denser mixed-use development. Fourth, the cultural preferences that underlie the organization of the Southern California region, particularly the sanctity of privatized space, may be more adaptable to constraints than previously
imagined. Environmental, traffic, and even social constraints may be accepted if they are seen as a way of preserving the essential freedoms of mid-

dle-class life-style. Fifth, the underlying strengths of a diversified, flexible, regional economy, deriving in part from the dispersed pattern of regional settlement and its inherent spatial flexibility, could provide increased social and
economic mobility for the poor.

A New Basis for the Public Realm

Each person, withdrawn into himself, behaves as though he is a
stranger to the density of others. His children and his good friends
constitute for him the whole of the human species. As for his transactions with his fellow citizens, he may be among them, but he sees
them not; he touches them, but does not feel them; he exists only in
himself and for himself alone. And if on these terms there remains in
him a sense of family, there no longer remains a sense of society.
—Alexis de Toqueville

In what follows it is argued that a concentration of value-oriented institutions, voluntary civic and community associations, combined with public
service institutions (e.g., education), constitute the seed that—planted in
mixed-use, higher density environments—will grow into a public realm. It is
a realm that would be decentralized at varying scales but structured to provide the basis for communal expression as public space. The mission of these
institutional centers would address the social, cultural, political, and environmental issues endemic to modern urban settlements. These concentrations of institutional infrastructures must be promoted by public policy and
investment and guided by the active participation of citizens.

The sense of an ordered society was once the precondition for the creation
of the public realm and its manifestation in intensely shared public space.
This older public realm is the expression of clear, though autocratic, political
and economic arrangements supported by once-shared institutional and religious values. The values and sensibility they engendered are in a state of dissolution, as Karl Marx understood:

Constant revolutionizing of production, uninterrupted disturbance
of all social relations, everlasting uncertainty and agitation, distinguish the bourgeois spark from all earlier times. All fixed, fact frozen
relationships, with their train of venerable ideas and opinions, are
swept away, all new formed ones become obsolete before they can
ossify. All that's solid melts into air. . . .

The democratic impulse toward freedom of personal expression, and the consequent proliferation of interest groups, is linked to the privatization of experience aggravated by the fear of change and the loss of control. Fundamentalist movements in politics and morals, the effort to reassert conservative values and re-root experience, are a compensating social reaction whose impact is further to disturb progressive social action across a broad spectrum. These processes are further destabilized by increased immigration and the proliferation of multi-ethnic populations. Robert McNiel of the University of Chicago comments:

> If we recognize this global breakup of traditional forms of rural life as the main feature of twentieth century history; then we may also see the competing ideologies and the rival alliances of our time as experiments in the management of populations that have been freed from the constraints of custom and that do not know what to expect under radically changing circumstances. Promises of accelerated economic development have an obvious appeal to land hungry peasants and ex-peasants who have migrated to cities in search of jobs. . . . Yet there is also a strong contrary current that seeks to restore the very sense of community, the shared values, that economic development weakens or destroys. Between the wars this took the form of nationalist and fascist movements, but it became theological after World War II as religious revivals—Jewish, Moslem, Christian, Hindu, and Buddhist—began to play important roles in world politics. . . . Thus today the tension between secular universalism . . . and religious sectarianism pervades the human response to the risk novelty inherent in the breakup of traditional orderings of society. . . .

Neither governmental reform nor private initiative operating through the market alone can be relied upon to restore a valid sense of community. Instead, we must look to an enhanced role for the voluntary associations that de Toqueville identified as a distinguishing characteristic of the American Revolution.

These civic and community agencies, supported by the focused intellectual resources of our universities and foundations, must learn to operate in the policy twilight between the powerful and well-funded single-purpose authorities and state, county, and local government. They are also uniquely suited to operating in the contingent realm of inter-ethnic relations, housing, education, citizen participation, and the environment, and participating in a variety of public policy debates. A whole new class of not-for-profit institutions is beginning to promote socially beneficial innovations in education, community-based policing, and environmental coalitions. It is estimated that

50% of the adult population of the country already spends over four hours a week working for nonprofit organizations.

In the Southern California region, the threats to the existing social order that may give impetus to collective public action through the voluntary sector may be summarized as follows.

Regional problems are interconnected. The most serious problems facing the viability of the region are interconnected, yet the agencies devised to address them are autonomous, fragmented, and organized around a single mission. Issues of transportation, land use, air quality, waste management, and housing are related, but never addressed as a system. As a result, agencies cross-plan, cross-regulate, and neutralize each other's initiatives. The friction arising from these inefficiencies also diverts large amounts of public funds that might otherwise be put to good use. Complex bureaucracies often cannot process funds allocated for large public works efficiently—leading to large unexpended reserves. Part of the public justification for the creation of authorities is the complex and technical nature of the problems being addressed (e.g., construction of mass transit), and the necessity of operating over time and across different political jurisdictions. The issue then becomes one of accountability. Civic associations, furnished with technically sophisticated advice from universities and elsewhere, are in the best position to represent the interests of the general public in holding these agencies accountable and advocating integrated planning among competing bureaucracies.

Environmental necessities will increasingly become a coercive force in the organization of public institutional strategies and will complicate debates over economic restructuring and job production. Regulatory issues and litigation associated with environmental impact reports threaten to compromise environmental quality by disturbing economic growth and stability. At the same time research is likely to broaden our understanding of the connection between pollution and public health, which will further intensify the debate. There is mounting evidence that environmental degradation may be related to the emergence of diseases resistant to public health strategies. Voluntary agencies offer the best hope of managing a dispute resolution process with the degree of disinterested sophistication necessary. Gore Vidal has called the environment the "green god" of the 21st century. Spiritual convictions arising from survival instincts will give compelling force to the social, economic, and political restructuring caused by environmental imperatives.

The *regional economic restructuring* now underway involves the internationalization of the economy, outsourcing of multiple subcontracts, the adjustment of the U.S. economy to competition, the impact of immigration, the growing importance of entertainment-related industries and the computer, and the reductions in standards of living that have partially promoted the mass entry of women into the work force. Public reaction takes the form of tax revolts, term limits, and an attack on bureaucracies and their costs, inflated by regulatory inefficiencies and the complexity of the problems they have to address. All these factors combine to create an environment in which there is less funding for public purposes.

The *social problems* facing the region have now twice erupted in civic violence at very substantial cost to the region as a whole. The nature of the conflicts underlying these disturbances are complicated by racism, police brutality, homelessness, the interaction of multiple ethnic cultures, the pattern and timing of immigrations, persistent and widening poverty, the decreasing spatial isolation of the poor from the middle class (and in some cases from each other), and the thrombosis in public education. The sensitivity and intimacy required to address these problems could arise from community-based organizations working with more broadly based civic institutions and universities to affect public policy and concerted private expenditures.

The *structure of the built environment* as it exists in Los Angeles now represents a paradigm for growth that already houses more than half of our population and is, with variations, the pattern of growth for most new urban settlements in the developed world. While it appears to provide a stimulating and perhaps necessary setting for economic trends, it also engenders environmental, social, and political problems that must be addressed at the regional level, where we are institutionally poor. The shape of the extended city is the consequence of deep forces of self-determination rooted in the spirit of modern democratic culture, which are likely to be accelerated by advances in the application of the computer to business communication, education, and entertainment.

Finally, *fragmentation and privatization,* however deeply rooted in our culture, however amplified by the fear of change and reduced economic circumstance, must not prevent the emergence of compensating social purpose. The urgent threats to the public welfare are at some level understood, although their expression in tax revolts, term limits, the initiative process, and low voter turnouts are not productive ways to address the problem. Alternative forms of participation are offered through the enhanced role of voluntary institutions, environmental advocates, community housing corporations, cooperative banks and credit unions, adult education centers, dispute resolution services, and private social services networks. These offer the best hope for establishing some elements of a binding consensus, of a community of trust, which permits public business to go forward without the proliferating litigation that is the most destructive expression of private protectionism. If there is hope in the intractable problems faced by regional communities around the nation, it lies in the edge of desperation most citizens feel, and in the collective fear of threats to our well-being as a community. Some will retreat behind privatized fundamentalist barricades; others may exercise their instinct for survival through participation and communal action.

The Morphology of a Public Realm

The character of public space associated with these proposed transformations will not follow historical models. Something approaching the scale of a village, or a loose collection of villages, would seem a more appropriate scale.

But the culture of unlimited choice and unconstrained growth, movement, and inflated freedoms now faces the prospect of being radically altered by the restructuring of the national and international economy, by the migrations of people from less-developed nations, by population growth, and by environmental limits. These developments constitute a new basis for the spatial expression of a collective impulse—the precondition of the public realm.

Our public spaces will not naturally take the shape of pure geometric form, implying a perfect, impossible, consensus, or alternatively, a singular authority unconstrained by democratic opinion. Instead, public space would take an opportunistic, pragmatic (convenient) shape, patched together from leftover spaces and negotiated contributions from private and public owners, compromised with messy edges, imperfect, surprising in idiosyncrasy, mixing solids and voids in ambiguous relation, but nevertheless possessing a public character through shared, connected space, coherent greenery tied to gardens, enhanced public circulation, and the penetration of these spaces into the body of private and institutional buildings through courtyards and glass-covered passages. Private or commercial frontages on public space should be permeable, presenting surfaces hollowed out at a public scale, or projecting in pavilions, to diminish the sense of uniform order, providing an expression of the private deferring to public necessities. Behind and above a shared, differentiated, mixed-use public base, private space should be allowed security and identity. Institutional buildings would be given prominence of position and treatment. A variety of institutions that address the needs of continuing education, job training, and day-care would be provided with subsidized locations.

The overwhelming presence of environmental necessities and constraints must also have a central metaphorical presence in the communities we build and in the way we build them, providing an architectural principle analogous

to the organizing presence of the church in European public space. These
constraints will increasingly impact built form, institutional and political
mission, and the poetic imagination. Space should therefore be provided for
the transformation of the public green of our colonial village heritage into
playing fields, gardens, and community agricultural space, reflecting an understanding that we must live with nature in reciprocal balance through cultivation, rather than either stand in awe and ecstasy or dominate in conquest
and spoilation.

These urban villages and boulevards will be distinct from the prevailing interstitial tissue of the region that will remain hinterland and incubator, too
vast in size and complexity to permit considered intervention. This tissue will
receive the first impact of immigrations, suffer from inter-ethnic tensions,
and represent a relatively unstable, even volatile social condition. In those
places of enhanced activity supported by transit, the sense of security will be
provided by the influence of benign value-oriented institutions with a communal mission, and communal experience. It is these voluntary institutions
that will increasingly mediate among ethnic subcultures and move between
the political and private sectors to reduce social conflict, improve education,
and articulate and promote the commonalities of interest that bind the citizenry to a sense of common purpose. From these settlements, civic colonies
can be established in the hinterlands and industrial mulch where waste,
decay, change, innovation, and new growth begins.

Conclusion

In reflecting on the implications of Los Angeles for urban settlement policy,
several themes emerge for which those of us who care about such things
seem dangerously ill-prepared. They arise from emerging forces so powerful
and little understood that effective policy interventions are difficult to imagine. Broadly speaking they are the result of population growth and migration,
the transformation of the global economy and the attenuation of the number
of jobs due to technology, health and resource problems arising from the
degradation of the environment, the privatization of experience and the at-
tendant and related growth of personal entertainment and fantasy promoted
by the computer, the dissolution of tradition and value systems that supported the idea of a collective good, the rise of fundamentalist political and
religious movements, and the alienation of most from the political process
and governance.

The most complete urban situation to have absorbed the early impacts of all these forces, and to have expressed their consequences, is Los Angeles. Significantly, entertainment (all media and themed productions) linked to the computer will soon surpass defense as the largest U.S. export. The creative community of Los Angeles is imbedded in the most diversified manufacturing base containing the highest concentration of high-tech industries in the country. The region also is likely to have the greatest number of sweatshops and the largest underground economy in the nation, and the greatest continued and growing potential for social unrest linked to poverty.

An approach to understanding the behavior of such a system, soon to involve a population of 20 million people, where over 150 languages are spoken, is only possible at a regional scale. And such an understanding is impossible without identifying the reciprocal relationship between the physical structure of the region and its behavior as a social, economic, and cultural system. The urgency and relevance of humanist ideals as they are formulated in current urban theory, especially by architects and urban designers, seem hopelessly inadequate, if not irrelevant, to the power and energy of the forces shaping places like Los Angeles around the world.

A kind of uncertainty principle should affect the attitude of urban designers and planners as they approach the problems of the extended city and its characteristic matrix. For to gain influence over a part of the built environment, we must leave the rest of it to other influences that are moved by social and economic forces we neither understand well nor have the power to control. Experience has taught that the dreams of urban paradise breed monsters, and that sometimes in wishing to eliminate what is messy, perceived as ugly, or despised as the consequence of greed, to eliminate poverty and injustice, or rather to rely solely on a rational system premised on an idealized concept of man, we produce results even more terrible than the circumstances that at first inspired comprehensive reform.

A democratic, pluralistic society generates imperfect partial plans. A necessary uncertainty is structured into the process, as a consequence of necessary compromise. As it is impossible to address social ills comprehensively, they will be addressed according to what is perceived as most urgent, within a context of competing alternative needs. Therefore, there will always be an unstructured, uncertain, ambiguous context of opportunity and despair in which specific action takes place. There will be a changing, imperfect matrix that persists, the behavior of which will occasionally produce a benefit that we may secure and amplify, or a misery too urgent to be ignored. Beneficial changes are most likely to occur when policy is able to focus these transforming energies around an existing potential to produce a new social circumstance, restructured institutional arrangements, and the physical correlative with which they interact and through which they are reinforced and a public realm established.

These places would express the inclination toward common purpose repressed in the structure of the extended city by the force of individual self-determination that separated us from Europe and its history. These beginnings will first exist within a larger fabric still compelled to take its shape from the idea of nature, privatized human settlement, and the practical, empirical imagination. Released by scientific inquiry and its technological successes to result in the conquest of a continent, we have elevated self-enrichment over a moral commonwealth, and promoted the dominance of convenient, private choice at the expense of social and community values.

Compensating adjustments must begin to be made to this system of culturally determined inclinations and the physical frame for our lives that is its built expression. Nature itself, and our social constructions, have begun to rebel against its operation; even the practical genius of our people is confounded by the uncontrolled complex interactions of its autonomous competing systems. Increasing social, economic, and environmental constraints will necessarily limit, are already limiting, the very freedom of action and dreams of self-fulfillment that attracted us west to this terrible and yet compelling and sometimes still beautiful place.

Toronto and Its
Metropolitan Region

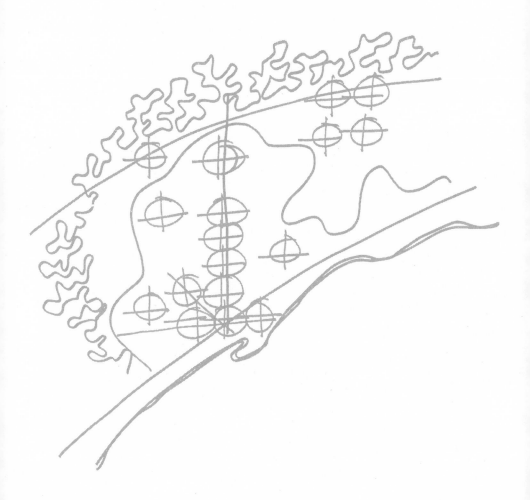

In their case study of Toronto and its metropolitan region, Gardner Church, Kenneth Greenberg, and Marilou McPhedran bring perspectives from government and urban policy studies, law and community advocacy, and architecture and urban design. Together, they explain the Toronto achievement—a balance of economy, environment, and social equity.

On the North American continent, Toronto is an alternative model for urban growth and form. The clearest comparison is with the extended growth pattern of Los Angeles. In contrast, Toronto has created social, economic, and physical intensification in *centers*, diversifying land uses and avoiding population segregations. The "vertical mosaic" of Toronto's multicultural population is a source of community support for people in everyday life. If one were to map the locations of the minorities, the poor, the elderly people in Toronto, the patterns would be very different from the typical patterns of other cities—as a result of public policies. For example, Toronto created the continent's largest stock of distributed mixed-income social housing. Toronto is a more equitable city because of the Canadian social safety net and tradition of social programming.

The vitality of the pedestrian-friendly downtown and the strength of the neighborhoods as places of social action remain Toronto's greatest bulwarks against systemic inequalities. While economic poverty remains, it is not concentrated in its built form. Toronto is slum-free.

Both social equity and environmental health were facilitated by the Toronto urban form that was built until the mid-1970s. Pedestrian networks and transit frameworks enabled a strong community fabric to prosper, and they retarded the land-consuming and smog-producing dependence on the automobile. Toronto built centers, linked by public infrastructure, like pearls on a string.

Toronto managed its post-war boom by creating a system of governance that integrated urban and suburban decision-making. For example, Metro Toronto built a network of infrastructure financed by the core city. The structured urban form had great social and environmental value. But, now, this Toronto tradition is threatened. Recently developed sprawl, representing half the population of the city-region, has few of the governmental, social, environmental, and spatial features that have made Toronto such a hopeful urban model.

Toronto: An Urban Alternative

Gardner Church, Kenneth Greenberg, and Marilou McPhedran

Toronto is often hailed as a North American urban anomaly. It is a safe, clean, and healthy city, with a vibrant urban core and a strong, diversified economy. But recent cracks have developed in this veneer of urban success, and now many Torontonians are wondering if their urban future is in jeopardy.

This case study examines the unique urban successes and pathologies of the Toronto region within the context of:

1. *Urban structure.* Toronto's distinctive governance structure has become fragmented, and several governance solutions are proposed.

2. *Urban form.* Three "transects" analyze Toronto's industrial, urban, and suburban dynamic.

3. *Community building.* A survey of a number of projects and initiatives aimed at perpetuating Toronto as a "healthy city."

Toronto's Urban Structure

Toronto consists of a metropolitan region surrounded by four offshoot regions and coupled with 35 lower tier municipalities. The regional and city governments split responsibility for municipal services. Generally the regions handle policing, ambulances, solid waste management, pollution control, social services, public transit, and regional roads. Cities take care of fire, water, local streets, development control, public health, and garbage collection. Each has a sometimes conflicting role in providing public housing, parks, economic development, and planning.

Toronto is Canada's center of capital and trade, but it is also the most multicultural city in the world according to the United Nations. More than 66

93

ethnic communities reside there, and over 100 languages are spoken. This is not surprising since for every two immigrants who have emigrated to Canada, one of them has settled in Toronto. Toronto's population will rise by nearly 50% over the next 25 years; most of this increase will come from immigration.

Toronto has also been blessed with a very high standard of living—one of the highest on the continent according to the United Nations Human Development Index. It lacks the physical ghettos of other cities, and, even in Toronto's public housing projects, the housing stock remains in relatively good shape and the reality of place is maintained.

Toronto's city core enjoys a high population density, mainly because of the pedestrian culture that developed in tandem with rapid transit in the 1900s. Unfortunately, in the last 50 years many of Toronto's city core residents have migrated to the suburbs. It is now a dense, transit-oriented core surrounded by a rainbow of automobile-dependent suburbs.

Still Toronto continues to enjoy one of the most livable downtowns in North America. There is a high level of intercourse among the suburbs and downtown. And this livability has allowed Toronto to build other suburban centers without—until very recently—worrying about the stability of the core.

Threats

Toronto is threatened on a number of fronts. One consistent worry is that as the national and provincial governments wrestle with their debts, Toronto may lack the public resources to meet its needs. Toronto is the single largest contributor to the gross national product, representing about 50% of the provincial tax base and about 25% of the national tax base. But despite its importance to the fiscal bottom line, Toronto has not seen that money flow back to meet its needs.

The city core, as mentioned earlier, is also under threat. This is partly due to the 1991 recession, which crippled the dominant financial, insurance, and real estate sectors. The city core also suffers from hundreds of acres of abandoned industrial land that lie vacant due to stringent environmental regulations and high redevelopment costs.

Toronto's main threat, however, flows from a crisis of governance. To understand that crisis it is necessary to look at the evolution of government in Toronto.

Governance Challenges in Toronto

In Canada local governments are under the complete control of the provincial government. Once a local government is created there is nothing—including referenda—available to protect municipalities from the provincial mandate.

In 1953 Toronto was reformed fundamentally, as the provincial government prepared for the growth pressures of the baby-boom and post-war immigration. The creation of the Municipality of Metropolitan Toronto (Metro) established one of North America's strongest urban planning frameworks. This framework was based on rapid transit (particularly subways), the rigorous preservation of public spaces, and a clear definition of the public domain. The result was a compact, pedestrian-friendly, major urban center.

In 1972 the Ontario government once again realized that urban growth was bridging Metro's boundaries and verging into the suburbs. The province considered expanding Metro's boundaries, but instead created a plan called "Design for Development," which contained three fundamental reforms: (1) a growth management plan, (2) municipal tax reform, and (3) the creation of four regional municipalities to surround the Municipality of Metropolitan Toronto.

Only cne of these reforms was delivered: the creation of the four regions. The problc m was that four powerful local governments were put in place, guided by neither a growth management strategy nor tax reform. So, instead of growing from a pedestrian- and transit-centered city, the Toronto region suddenly discovered the realities of urban sprawl and the real estate industry.

The Governance Crisis

The forthcoming wave of government reform must go farther than the reforms of 1953 or 1972. At the bare minimum the growth management plan and municipal tax reform promised two decades ago must be introduced. If that does not happen, Toronto will not be ready for the growth challenges of the next two decades.

But the provincial ministries that have the power to make municipal change do not work together. They exist in "vertical silos," focused solely on narrowly defined mandates. Hence, cross-jurisdictional problems are either missed, deemed unsolvable, or approached in a haphazard fashion. It is important to look at how this lack of integration affects the economic, environmental, and social aspects of the region.

Economists say that competition occurs not among countries but among major cities. Livable, safe cities with a clean environment and relative ease of mobility tend to attract and maintain economic activity. The economy of Toronto is usually a barometer for the economy of the nation. But the economic ministries of the Canadian and Ontario governments virtually ignore the Toronto economy because of the fragmentation noted above.

All major social issues are urban. These include racial harmony, public safety, child welfare, education, gender equity, and family violence. Therefore, the major social challenges facing Canada will only be resolved in Toronto, Montreal, and Vancouver. If the major urban areas become socially harmonious places, the society will be peaceful and successful; if they fail, Canadian society will suffer. But no government sees, let alone manages, the urban place as the key to social harmony.

Also, urban dwellers have the greatest opportunity to contribute to environmental sustainability. They can reduce automobile use, move away from free-standing heating and air conditioning, and reform their waste and water management practices. But Toronto's governmental systems are not designed to marshall their citizens toward a healthy environment.

A New Policy Instrument?

The environmental, social, and economic challenges faced by a community cannot be addressed as separate "boxes" of issues. Unless we create a government that integrates equity, environment, and economy on every issue it addresses—we will fail as a society.

A new Toronto could set an example for Canada. For example, a holistic policy group should be at the center of a new government structure. This policy group would examine each policy issue for its effect on environment, social equity, and economy. The group would consult with specialists, each of whom would be "on tap"—specialized counsel—but not "on top"—no direct control over policy setting. This holistic policy group would also take and give information and direction from and to Toronto's communities.

Five Principles for a New System of Toronto Government

Five principles should guide the creation of Toronto's new system of urban government.

The first is *policy holism*. The policy framework for urban regions should cover the entire urban region. It should integrate land use, environment, quality of life, poverty, and education.

The second principle is *subsidiarity*. This insists that public administration be as close to the community as possible, provided there is sufficient scale for service delivery. For example, from the vantage point of a neighborhood block, it is easy to foretell transportation problems when a city considers an end to street parking; at the metropolitan level that is not so obvious.

The third principle is *particularity*. North America has mastered the art of the municipal act that covers all purposes, all regions, and all cities. The problem is that neither the urban region nor the broader area benefits from an appropriate policy environment. Instead, governance should fit the unique circumstances of each area. The only exception might be when a broader policy is founded on human rights or other recognized standards.

The fourth principle demands *relief for the urban taxpayer*. Urban regions continue to share resources with rural regions to a greater extent in Canada than in the United States. Policymakers have believed rightly that poverty in Canada's rural areas should be alleviated, but often this happens without relieving urban poverty. We need to ensure that revenue raised in cities is transferred only when poverty levels are higher outside the city. Reducing public spending also helps set an adequate tax level without creating new debt.

The final principle is *coherence*. Governance must be understood by the electorate. Confusion breeds indifference and apathy, which provide the ideal atmosphere for corruption and demagoguery. Also, tinkering with the present system is not an acceptable way of creating coherence.

Structural Options for Governance in the Toronto Region

These principles can apply to many governmental models. These are just five, any of which would maintain Toronto's tradition of developing new approaches to address growth and social change.

The City-State

A city-state creates a new subnational entity with all of the responsibility of a province or state. This is a good model for Europe (Rotterdam is the best example) but seems counter to the political culture of North America. If, however, our respective fiscal crises worsen, the city-state model might become feasible, especially in cities like New York or Canada's National Capital Region (Ottawa-Hull) that straddle one or more state or provincial boundaries.

A Group of Regional Municipalities

In the Toronto context this would divide our 5 million people into several good-sized regional municipalities and abolish the dozens of existing cities. A provincial office would coordinate these regional municipalities. This model might work very effectively, provided that the number of regional municipalities is kept reasonably small.

A Region of Cities

This model has had the most discussion in Toronto. The five regional municipalities would disappear, and in their place a single Greater Toronto Region would coordinate some 35 smaller cities. This model might work in theory, but it clashes with Ontario's and Toronto's political cultures, as it would with those of many American cities where the urban–suburban identity is even more pronounced.

A Region of Communities

In this model a region would be created with virtually all municipal powers. Dozens of small communities or neighborhoods would be incorporated under this region. Each community would represent itself to the region but would have only meager responsibility for local government. Democracy might thrive under this model of powerful local politics and a powerful regional government. Accountability, however, might suffer since the bureaucracy would be controlled by a cadre of regional administrators.

Several Regions of Communities

This concept might be useful for Toronto. The current five regions would remain, but they would deliver all provincial and municipal services. This would be very similar to the "region of cities" model, but rather than an internal structure of cities, it would have an internal structure of neighborhoods or communities. A new provincial ministry would provide holistic policy and standards as it coordinated the five regions, but both subsidiarity (all provincial services would be delivered by the regions) and policy holism (integrated transportation, land use, and environmental management) would be satisfied.

The Golden Report

In January 1996, Dr. Anne Golden presented the final report of The Task Force on the Future of the Greater Toronto Area (GTA). Dr. Golden and four others were appointed in April 1995 to respond to growing concerns about the health and workability of the Toronto region. The Golden Task Force's final report saw the following as critical issues:

- pooling of commercial and industrial property tax assessment;
- replacement of the five existing regional governments with a single Greater Toronto Council; and
- giving local municipalities added powers and responsibilities.

At this time the provincial government is assessing the Golden Report.

The Role of Large Cities

The future of Canadian society is based on an understanding of the role of large cities. Government structure, however, is simply the first step toward this understanding. If we can find the capacity to empower the appropriate form, then the region or regions will have to ensure good urban form. The next section explores Toronto's urban form experience.

Toronto's Urban Form

A *transect* is an area of land that is marked off and then observed over time. Transects have been used by botanists, and later by ecologists, to track the life of a discrete section of forest, field, or wetland.

Recently transect studies have been applied to urban settings. The demography, land use, and historic settlement patterns observed in just a few blocks can tell much about the broad urban form of a major city. We have chosen three linear transects in the Toronto region to describe the area's urban form.

1. an east-west strip along the Lake Ontario waterfront;
2. a north-south strip, the Yonge Street corridor; and,
3. an east-west strip, along the Highway 7 corridor.

These transects indicate the origins of our urban form. They also show areas of opportunity as well as some of Toronto's historical pathologies.

The Waterfront Transect

This transect is several kilometers wide and stretches some 28 kilometers along Toronto's Lake Ontario waterfront. From its earliest days Lake Ontario, and the rivers which run into it, have defined Toronto's urban form.

The waterfront is also where Toronto's vision has clashed with pragmatism. For instance, in the late 1800s city politicians began to dream of a pedestrian esplanade along the shoreline of Lake Ontario. But with the advent of the railway this "esplanade" became the perfect place to develop a rail corridor. Thus the residents of the city became separated from their waterfront via a trade-off with commerce.

Industrial development continued along this transect throughout the first half of the 20th century. With the post-war boom of the 1950s, however, automobile traffic began to clog the area's roads.

In the early 1950s, planners from the new Municipality of Metropolitan Toronto began working on the Gardiner Expressway. This six-lane elevated expressway runs parallel to the railway corridor along the waterfront. Like the railway, the Gardiner Expressway brought further prosperity and isolation to the waterfront.

In the 1960s the heavy industry along the waterfront began migrating to the suburbs. The railways soon followed, transferring their rail freight operations to areas north of the city. This industrial and railway migration freed up valuable downtown land for other more intensive urban uses.

In the early 1970s the government of Canada bought an 80-acre abandoned waterfront property, which became known as Harbourfront. From the start Harbourfront has had financial problems even though it draws some 3 million visitors per year. But, this development has evolved with mixed success into a recreational, cultural, residential, and commercial urban park. Also, along with the condominium and hotel projects that sprouted in the late 1970s, Harbourfront has accelerated a major reurbanization or "recycling" of vacant waterfront lands.

Waterfront reurbanization has also touched the Garrison Common area of the waterfront, just west of the downtown core. This area enjoys a rich industrial and recreational heritage and is home to beer, clothing, and farm equipment producers, as well as Canada's annual national exhibition. Much of the industry has now left the Garrison Common area, and steps are being taken to develop residential and commercial communities (particularly through a 1 million-square-foot international trade center). The current challenge in the Garrison Common area is the ability to decontaminate, reconfigure, and reuse vast tracts of obsolescent but strategically located territory. This includes the introduction of street, block, and service infrastructure.

To a large extent, the Waterfront Regeneration Trust is responsible for the transformation of the Toronto waterfront. This provincially supported special purpose body acts as an information clearinghouse, project coordinator, and advocate for an ecological approach to the Lake Ontario waterfront and watershed. Its existence also shows the public sector's role in shaping Toronto's urban form.

The North-South Yonge Street Transect

Yonge Street is the historic north-south spine of Toronto. While it is no longer the geographic center of the region, the street still serves as a dividing line between Toronto's west and east. Yonge Street has also served as Toronto's transit corridor, with the resulting concentration of urban and commercial areas all within walking distance of Yonge Street.

The southern end of the Yonge transect features Toronto's characteristic mix of housing types and incomes. Much of this diversity is due to the fine-grained street grid that was developed in the early part of this century. The grid let lower and upper income earners build houses back to back, sharing blocks and lane ways. This mix of peoples continued into the post-war era as different immigrant communities settled next to one another.

In the 1970s the city of Toronto created a new mixed-income community known as the St. Lawrence neighborhood just east of Yonge. Here medium-density cooperative and nonprofit apartments were built next to the railway lands. This development succeeded because of an urban design strategy that revived Toronto's earlier pattern of streets and blocks, as well as imaginative architectural design.

A few blocks north we find the "Yonge Street strip." This area features a mix of high-density retail (including Toronto's principal tourist attraction, the Eaton Centre) as well as three theaters and one of Toronto's universities. This once-decaying area was home to prostitution, drugs, and crime in the 1960s and 1970s. While it retains some of its past vices, streetscape improvements, some key economic development projects, and the added life flowing from the two musical theaters have brought people back to the area.

Intensification continues up Yonge Street, especially at most major subway stops. During the boom in the 1970s and 1980s, little attention was paid to integrating new office and residential buildings into the older surrounding neighborhoods. Now, with a 16% commercial vacancy rate, many of the office towers are being transformed into low-cost condominiums. Hence, the residential character of Toronto's core is being preserved due to the soft market for office space. Here, as in the Waterfront transect, land is recycled and reused. The emphasis, though, is on strategic infill and retrofitting a well-established urban structure.

A significant urban node has formed along the northern part of Yonge Street between Highway 401 and the North York civic center. This area has seen intense commercial and residential development, as employment centers have shifted to older suburban centers. This has affected both the live/work relationship and transportation patterns, since work trips get shorter when there are more areas of work.

Finally, this transect intersects with the northern edge of the Toronto area, where the low-density, automobile-dependent suburbs begin.

The Northern Fringe Transect

Toronto's northern suburban development is constrained by the Oak Ridges glacial moraine, a provincially protected ecological feature that contains the headwaters of several rivers and streams. Still, even though the suburbs cannot grow to the north, east-west expansion continues, driven by both housing demand and expansion of the highway system.

In the 1960s Toronto formed the suburban community of Don Mills, a hybrid of the low-density, automobile-dependent American suburb and British new-town planning. In the 1970s, after "Design for Development" recommended the five urban regions, a unique consortium of Canada's large banks, a few major developers, and the newly powerful regional governments built dozens of simplified Don Mills clones. The public wanted both affordability and a modified version of the American dream; they got it in suburban Toronto. Now thousands of single-family dwellings occupy some of Canada's richest agricultural lands.

Fortunately, the lessons of three decades of urban sprawl are guiding new developments along this transect. The Town of Markham, for example, is home to several compact developments modeled on the urban form of the central core. Each of these small developments will have the same density as three or four traditional suburban developments, allowing for a better quality of community life and reduced sprawl. Also, some suburban nodes, such as Scarborough's Town Centre, are becoming more urban. Here a diversity of residential, institutional, civic, and commercial areas thrive, thanks to their proximity to rapid transit lines

These examples of suburban transformation give some hope of creating a better urban place. But the automobile continues to vex any massive change in suburban growth management. For example, the spine that defines this northern edge transect is a new provincial toll highway that is currently under construction. It seems that Toronto still maintains a degree of cognitive dissonance between the trade-offs of creating compact urban form and a continuing reliance on the automobile.

A brief look at the three transects tells something about the urban form and the general story of Toronto, but also about the differences among three parts of the region.

In summary, the Waterfront transect's major challenge is the ability to decontaminate, reconfigure, and reuse vast tracts of obsolescent but strategically located territory. In the Yonge Street transect the established urban pattern remains generally unchanged, with a vibrant, residential city core. Along the Northern Fringe, however, we see the beginnings of a shift from a suburban model to a more intensified urban form. The success of the entire urban region depends on doing all three activities simultaneously.

Changes to the governance structure and to urban form suggest ways that our city-region can adjust to growth pressures. There must also be fundamental changes in the way we function as communities if our city is to thrive.

Community Building in Toronto

The previous two sections outline the work that has gone into the urban structure and form of the Toronto area. The same intensity is being poured into Toronto's "Healthy Communities" model.

Toronto's experience in building a healthy community is rooted in other visionary models and concepts. In the 1870s, Dr. Benjamin Ward Richardson pioneered Britain's "Public Health Act," which included measures that would ameliorate the death and disease of the urban poor. Some 100 years later, the World Health Organization stated that health is the extent to which an individual or group is able to realize aspirations, satisfy needs, and change or cope with the environment. Health is a positive concept that emphasizes social and personal resources, as well as physical capacity.

This broad definition of health, coupled with the vision and activism of over a century ago, has suggested a new approach to urban health. It suggests that community health has a demonstrative effect on urban and national economic and social well-being. It also indicates that health is more than the absence of disease and involves the connection among a variety of social, economic, environmental, and personal resources.

Paradigm Shift

The section on urban structure suggested that a new approach is needed to reconnect Toronto's fiscal, economic, social, and governmental structures. Part of this new approach may be a change in the way bureaucracies gauge efficiency and success. In the past the bureaucrats focused on getting to "yes"—the ends rather than the means. Now the entire process is seen as a measure of success, partly in terms of how process can respond quickly, but also how it involves people in integrating equity, economy, and environment.

The zero-sum game of calculating winners and losers no longer works in a complex world. But internally, as people begin to understand that the ways of thinking and doing have changed, they begin to better anticipate change. This anticipation—the emergence of lateral thinking—creates even more successes. Also, it is ironic that the first groups to identify necessary change are those that society would consider to be "outsiders." Therefore systems and leaders must remain open to the perspectives of the unelected, unheard, unknown, or unseen members of society.

These aspects of a paradigm shift on ideas of social success and urban health have guided the creation of a "Healthy Communities" model for the Toronto area. They have also driven the work of the city of Toronto's Healthy City Office (HCO).

Toronto's Healthy City Office

The HCO works as a broker but also a catalyst, setting broad agendas that blossom into feasible projects at the street and neighborhood level. For example, the HCO led a Clean Air Partnership among four public and private sector partners. This resulted in a number of pilot projects, as well as a city bylaw against idling automobiles. Similarly, the HCO's Homeless Persons Self-Help project led to the creation of a Woman's Community Economic Development Network.

The lessons learned by the Healthy Cities Office have assisted many community development projects in the Toronto area. Each project:

- features a mix of partners, though the public sector is always one of them;

- is multisectoral (universities, hospitals, community-based organizations, businesses, and governments);

- is multijurisdictional (involvement is sought from the city, regional, provincial, and federal levels of government);

- is multidisciplinary (different training and approaches—from architecture and public health to public works and planning); and

- follows an inclusive, "bottom-up" approach (the people involved in the problem—e.g., prostitutes, the homeless, youth gangs—are involved early in the process and therefore invest in its success).

Projects and Initiatives

Toronto Islands Community

The Toronto Islands are a natural archipelago formed at the mouth of the Don River along the Lake Ontario shoreline. People have lived and played on the islands throughout Toronto's history, but problems arose when the Municipality of Metropolitan Toronto was formed. Metro controlled the services that supported the island residential community, such as water, sewer, and hydro. It also controlled the parkland that was adjacent to the island's residential area. Metro Toronto seemed to regard island residents as virtual squatters and became determined to transform the entire island area into parkland.

The islanders responded by creating a community council. This council guarded against Metro eviction efforts and also forged alliances with local politicians and mainland communities. In the end, the islanders saved their community and helped integrate public parklands into their residential areas. The result showed that formation of structured community councils can be a successful tactic in community conflicts.

Parkdale

Sixty years ago Parkdale was an area where wealthy Toronto residents lived, in proximity to both Lake Ontario and the central business district. In the early 1960s the new Gardiner Expressway began to isolate Parkdale, and the area changed from a rich to a poor neighborhood. But, during the late 1980s boom, young urban professionals moved in and began to discover the difficulties of raising families amid drug dealing and prostitution. Something needed to be done.

The lesson here is community empowerment. A series of community coalitions were formed, made up of citizens, local business people, government officials, and community workers. These community coalitions bypassed local politicians by directly approaching the media, as well as provincial, regional, and city officials. They have been successful because they created a consensus at a grassroots level.

Dufferin Mall

The area surrounding Dufferin and Lansdowne Avenues is a sibling of the troubled Parkdale area. The area enjoys tremendous ethnic diversity but has also suffered from drug trafficking among the many youth at risk who live in the area.

The Dufferin Mall was both a community landmark and the locus for much of the area's crime. But, rather than tighten security, David Hall, the Dufferin Mall manager, used his budget and position to encourage broad solutions to the community's problems. He donated space in the mall to local multicultural groups and worked with a neighboring high school to start a drop-in school for dropouts. The mall also staffed and funded a community newspaper to offer information as well as to develop a sense of local identity. Finally, Hall and his management staff developed merchant associations with the smaller local businesses—both inside and outside of the mall—to keep them aware of, and involved in, community building.

Jane/Finch Corridor

In the 1970s the federal government built new high-rise apartments to house low-income families in the vacant Jane Street and Finch Avenue area. As development crept around Jane/Finch, clashes between income and racial groups became inevitable. This area became the closest thing in Ontario to the "projects" of American cities.

The Jane/Finch experience has shown that building communities at an early stage is more cost-efficient than crisis-triggered interventions that cause enormous anxiety and offer little or no lasting value. The federal government has targeted children and youth for its funding. This support, however, is conditional on demonstrated cooperation and coordination among other agencies, including all four levels of government, Children's Aid, two Boards of Education, the police, and community leaders. Also, the Laidlaw Foundation, a major private-sector philanthropic organization, has become a financial partner through its Community Systems Partnership.

Street City

"Street City" is an imaginative approach to housing homeless people in a transitional facility. The imaginative aspect flows from bringing the target group—the many homeless people on the streets of Toronto—in as partners at an early stage, and therefore in having them make an investment in the efficacy of the project.

The project was built in an abandoned warehouse near the eastern waterfront, and it includes a meeting hall, dining areas, and laundry facilities. The building was designed to create self-contained "houses," a "main street," and recreational spaces. A "town council" was also formed from street people, as well as representatives of the community, local churches, and the city of Toronto. Within the Street City community, a group of homeless women have been working cooperatively on a quilt-making project. The proceeds from the sale of these quilts help to fund other projects, while also building confidence in the participants.

Support for Street City has come from a variety of fronts, including money from private, charitable, and public sources. Some of the financial motivation has come from those who are desperate about the numbers of homeless people, and who see Street City as an investment in "cleaning up the streets." Regardless of the funders' motives, the project has created a transitional place for homeless people and has instilled confidence in the Street City residents.

Common Lessons from Community Building in Toronto

A healthy community cannot be built without leadership. Each project referred to in this case study has benefitted from a public presence—through politicians, public officials, and public agencies. But each project would have fallen apart if dominance and control had been the rubric of leadership. The lesson here is that leadership does not equal control, any more than an efficient process must mean an exclusionary one. Another lesson is that healthy communities flow from the preservation of public goods, such as clean air, soil, and water; green space; safe streets; and effective schools.

Healthy community building stops when the global or holistic perspective gets separated from local action. People must be aware of their own community needs and also be motivated to govern themselves. Problems only develop when communities lose sight of the broader societal needs, and when empowerment leads to NIMBYism.

Finally, each community will strike its own balance among economy, equity, and environmental variables. This healthy communities model should not assign a conscience role to just one partner.

Conclusion

Three basic tenets differentiate Toronto's urban character from that of other North American cities. First, Toronto is the most multicultural city in the world, according to the United Nations. Second, throughout the city's modern history, coherent public policy for all parts of the urban area has been both possible and desirable. Finally, class segregation is not a factor in Toronto—moves toward income, housing, and community integration are the norm.

Still, this case study suggests that the Toronto region is at a crossroads. The area's urban structure is fragmented and therefore unable to meet the forthcoming fiscal and growth challenges. Toronto's urban form challenges are also resilient to change. Along the northern transect the dominant urban form is still highly regimented, stripped-down, automobile-dependent development. This reliance on the automobile contributes to air pollution and forces long commuting distances. Also, our attempts at building a healthy community are limited by shrinking budgets as well as the intractability of old paradigms and approaches. The area, however, is still livable, and it has not yet fallen prey to the urban pathologies of other major urban regions.

Toronto's urban form has diversified land use and encouraged intensification (especially in the Yonge Street and Waterfront areas). The result has been a much more lively and vital urban center than that of most of Toronto's American counterparts.

The traditional suburban form is also being challenged. There are moves to create a mix of housing and employment in intensified developments along the edge of Toronto's urban area. Simultaneously many older suburban nodes are beginning to mimic higher density urban patterns, especially along transit lines. Also, many areas are forging better links between economic opportunities and the available labor force through nodal employment centers.

We have regions with (1) strong municipal mandates, (2) deep debt capacity, and (3) a very strong tradition of public administration. We also have governance options as well as a history of making major successful government reforms. We have adjusted to economic and demographic changes without irreparably damaging the urban fact of our downtown core. And, finally, we know how to build communities, by directing energies, resources, and know-how to areas and groups in need.

The future is still in question, but not in jeopardy.

Acknowledgments

The authors wish to thank the following for their assistance with the preparation of this case study: John MacMillan, freelance writer and editor; Robert Wright, Centre for Landscape Research, University of Toronto; and Dan Burns, Deputy Minister, Ontario Ministry of Municipal Affairs and Housing.

New York City and the New York Region

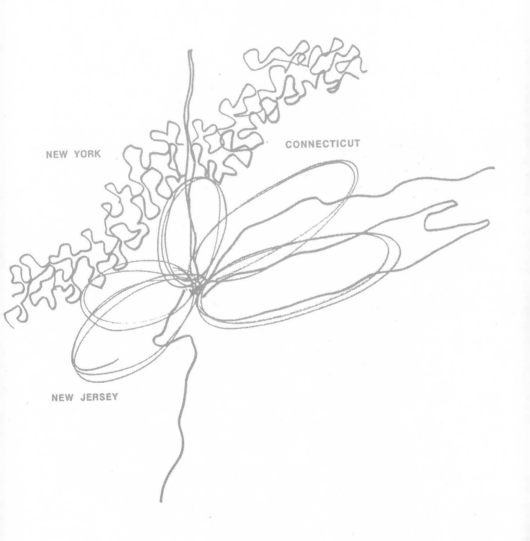

NEW YORK

CONNECTICUT

NEW JERSEY

In their case studies of New York, Jonathan Barnett (an architect and urban designer) and Robert D. Yaro and Thomas K. Wright (urban and regional planners) bring different perspectives on the history and future of New York. But, in the end, their viewpoints overlap: the authors of both case studies see New York as a *city-region*.

The growth and form of New York is indicative of the emergence of city-regions. New York originally had a single core, Lower Manhattan. As it grew outward, it was joined by outer boroughs—for example, Brooklyn—and it developed a second, even larger, business district in Midtown Manhattan. By the mid 20th century, the growth and form of New York—a series of concentric rings around Manhattan—began to change. A new form of urban development evolved—a series of overlapping subregions, like the petals of a flower. Each of the petals have their own identity—like Long Island or New Jersey—with centers of their own, but they also continue to share the original center, Manhattan.

But there are risks. New York's growth and form has resulted in social equity problems, some new, some old. Barnett, for example, points out that the 1930s interventions of Robert Moses, "divided the city physically in unprecedented ways; these physical divisions accentuated social divisions." Later, Barnett points out, the 1960s spreading city was accompanied by "the serious destabilization and deterioration in older low- and moderate-income neighborhoods." Now, there is the risk of spatial divorce, possibly racial, ethnic, and class polarization, between "affluent, separate new cities that have effectively severed their connections" with the inner city and the inner suburbs.

Similarly, the new Third Regional Plan of New York points out that "the extreme deconcentration of North America's metropolitan regions has played havoc with the green infrastructure...that makes life in these places possible and desirable."

To meet these challenges, Yaro and Wright set forth a conception of the city-region based on the three E's (economy, environment, and equity) embodied in proposals for regional greenswards to conserve environmental resources; the creation and restoration of many kinds of urban *centers* and growth *boundaries,* to counteract the sprawl of the region; and the creation of mobility linkages that effectively serve the economy and environment of the region.

City Design and the Development of New York City

Jonathan Barnett

═══

Historical Background

New York City became an important metropolis because of its harbor, more accessible and closer to Europe than Philadelphia or Baltimore, more central to the eastern seaboard than Boston. The Erie Canal, built between 1817 and 1824, connected the Hudson River to the Great Lakes, shaping the development of the whole state of New York and preserving the Port of New York's competitive advantages as the United States expanded westward. New York City maintained its position in the railroad age, although New York's islands and waterways created a problem for railroads, and later for highways.

New York has always been a mercantile city. It was only briefly the national capital; it isn't even the state capital. The Commissioner's Plan of 1811 explicitly rejected the grand civic design of Washington, D.C., or the more moderate ambitions of Buffalo and Detroit, in favor of a street grid that provided the most efficient access to the largest number of building lots.

The city grew rapidly, with growth intensifying during and after the Civil War. New York became a low, soot-stained place with tightly packed, five-story tenements and row after row of brownstone houses. Industry was supported by surges of immigration beginning in the 1840s. New York was the major port of entry; and, while most immigrants moved on to other parts of the United States, New York became the city of many nationalities that it still is today.

Rapid growth led to the next significant city design initiative in New York—the reservation of Central Park, replacing a shantytown and just ahead of the northward movement of real estate development. Central Park was followed by later reservations for Prospect Park in Brooklyn, Riverside Park, and other parks in Upper Manhattan and the Bronx. It is hard to imagine what the New York of unrelieved, speculative development would have looked like had these farsighted design decisions not been made.

The overcrowding and squalid conditions in the city's slums, as documented by Jacob Riis in *How the Other Half Lives,* led to tenement housing laws, the building of public baths, and the settlement houses created by private charities to help immigrants adjust to their new surroundings.

Around the turn of the 20th century subways began to extend or replace the elevated transit lines and street railways, linking residential districts to Lower and Midtown Manhattan. This improved transit network coincided with the consolidation of Manhattan and its four surrounding counties into New York City, bringing together the business centers and most of the suburbs at the time and making New York a regional city. The transportation network of this consolidated New York was centered on Lower Manhattan and Midtown, supporting the skyscrapers, which became, along with the electric signs in Times Square, New York's most significant design characteristics.

The tall buildings and growing industrialization led to the 1916 zoning ordinance, which—while it was not intended as a city design concept—had a major shaping effect on the denser portions of the city.

Other major city design initiatives of the first part of 20th century were inspired by the interventions made in Paris beginning in the 1850s, which had demonstrated how parks, boulevards, and other public works could make a city look and function better.

Developments comparable to those initiated under Napoleon III included improved railway connections and the creation of the two great railway passenger terminals (but not an equivalent system for rail freight); the building of Park Avenue and Riverside Drive in Manhattan, the Grand Concourse in the Bronx, and Eastern and Ocean Parkways in Brooklyn; major improvements to the city's water and sewer systems; and construction of the Manhattan, Williamsburgh, and Queensborough bridges.

Robert Moses, who directed the construction of public works in New York City from the 1930s through the mid-1960s, went beyond the Parisian model. The precedents for slum clearance and the replacement of slums with large-scale housing projects were largely English. They represent another stage in an evolving concept of the public interest. Moses also took the Parisian model for parks and boulevards up to the scale of the automobile. He created New York's highways, and their associated bridge and tunnel network, plus the regional park and recreation system, parts of which, like the grounds for the 1939 New York World's Fair, were within the city limits. These interventions, while they were logical extensions of previous ways of thinking about city improvement, divided the city physically in unprecedented ways; and these physical divisions accentuated social divisions.

Rockefeller Center, the first phase of which was completed during the Great Depression in the 1930s, is another landmark in the history of improving New York City—a design for a group of tall buildings, organized as a cluster, not as a series of street frontages.

Problems and Policies Since 1950

In 1950 the urbanized New York metropolitan area extended to bedroom communities far beyond the city boundaries, but the Manhattan business centers were still preeminent in the region; port activities lined the Manhattan and Brooklyn waterfronts; traditional manufacturing filled the industrial band along the East River; old-time residential neighborhoods were still intact. New York in 1950 had its problems: slums, old-law tenements, hideous elevated railroad lines, dirty and antiquated factories. But, in retrospect it had reached its peak of power and importance, symbolized by its selection as the headquarters location for the United Nations, making New York literally the capital of the world.

In a few years much of this power began to drain away. Corporate headquarters began to move to the suburbs and to other cities; the main part of the port was relocated to Port Elizabeth, New Jersey; industry began to leave; and the population of the older neighborhoods began to move out to new suburban housing, creating serious destabilization and deterioration in older low- and moderate-income neighborhoods.

At first the New York City establishment responded with more of the same type of city-design policies that had worked up to the 1950s: the New York World's Fair of 1964; more slum clearance; more massive housing projects like Co-op City and the first plans for Battery Park City; more highway construction, such as the Cross Bronx, Mid-Manhattan, and Lower Manhattan expressways; the Verrazano Bridge, and Rockefeller Center–style building group plans like Lincoln Center and the World Trade Center. In the meantime, traditional *laissez-faire* government permitted the demolition of Penn Station and the loss of many other valuable, historic buildings from the earlier, Paris-influenced phase of civic improvement.

In 1965 New York enacted a comprehensive revision of the city's 1916 zoning code, a reform that was well-intentioned but that institutionalized large-scale clearance of existing structures and project-like design for private buildings as well as public ones.

By the time John Lindsay became Mayor in 1966, it was clear that major changes were needed in city-design policies to meet changing conditions. In the next few years the city:

- Stopped slum clearance in favor of selective renewal of individual sites, and initiated neighborhood planning with community participation, code enforcement in neighborhood districts, housing rehabilitation, and "vest-pocket" parks and housing.
- Prepared urban design plans for complex and significant areas of the city: Midtown Manhattan, Lower Manhattan, downtown Brooklyn, and many neighborhoods.
- Abandoned the Mid-Manhattan and Lower Manhattan expressways.
- Introduced a new kind of highway planning integrating roads with parks and neighborhoods, including the ambitious plan for Westway, which ultimately was not built.
- Instituted commercial renewal policies in neighborhood shopping districts and in downtown Brooklyn, downtown Jamaica, and Fordham Road in the Bronx.
- Sought to make New York more competitive for conventions and tourism.
- Revised the new zoning code to get rid of its most damaging provisions, recognizing the complexity of Midtown and Lower Manhattan by creating special zoning districts.
- Created an active program to save the historic fabric of the city, including historic districts, the Landmarks Preservation Commission, and air-rights transfer districts.

While subsequent mayors have not been as supportive of urban design as Lindsay, the policies created at that time are still the city's urban design policies, and have led to considerable success:

- historic districts and landmark preservation;
- better design of important private buildings;
- acceptance of neighborhood planning (although the resources to complete the plans are not there);
- completion of special zoning districts like Times Square; and
- completion of development projects like Battery Park City and Roosevelt Island.

The Present Danger and Reasons for Hope

New York City today is in great danger. *New York City Ascendant, the Report of the Commission on the Year 2000,* instituted by Mayor Koch and published in 1987, proved to be a misjudgment that would be laughable if the complacency it epitomized had not been so pervasive. It is not that the Commission did not recognize the city's serious problems, but it wrote about them as if it were still 1965. It had little to say about new technologies that promote decentralization instead of the concentrated activity that has always been New York City's strongest asset. It ignored the effect on New York City of a generation of competing development in the metropolitan region, described by my colleagues Robert Yaro and Tom Wright in the following case study.

In many ways that the Commission on the Year 2000 refused to recognize, New York City's ability to control its own future has been taken out of its hands. The intensive commercial, manufacturing, and residential development in what used to be the suburbs has the potential to become even more self-sufficient than it is already. This development has created affluent, separate new cities that have effectively severed their connection with New York. In the meantime, New York could continue in a downward spiral of increasing social problems, decreasing resources with which to deal with them, continued departure of business and residents, increasing social problems, and so on. New York City's recent, well-publicized budget crises could be an indication of far worse troubles to come.

At the same time, New York City still has its competitive advantages. Manhattan's skyline of extraordinary towers, New York's great institutions and parks, the huge investment in existing buildings and infrastructure are all tremendous assets. New York continues to be a world financial center; its concentration of the arts, publishing, broadcasting, and advertising industries makes New York City a major provider of content for the new electronic means of communication as well as for older media. Immigration provides a continuing supply of energetic, ambitious people, many of whom these days come with a strong educational background and sometimes bring financial resources with them.

The rapid implementation of Battery Park City during the 1980s, the construction of the new Convention Center, the rebuilding of the Times Square area, the continuing investment in Soho, Manhattan's upper west side, the "big-box" retail on lower Sixth Avenue, and neighborhoods like Flushing, Astoria, and Ocean Parkway all show New York City's continued economic vitality.

While the city's financial troubles have meant continued cutbacks in essential services, private philanthropy has helped restore Central Park and other major parks; and private business improvement districts have picked up some of the maintenance and repair functions that financial stringency has prevented the city government from performing. The rejuvenation of Bryant Park is a good example of the successful implementation of a business improvement district. But in most Western European countries a similar level of investment is routinely provided by local government.

Despite all of New York City's problems, it is hard to walk through Midtown Manhattan, ride through Central Park, or drive up Park Avenue and imagine that New York City will not survive. Even in some of New York's most deteriorated areas, like the South Bronx, there are new rows of townhouses and other signs that the city has "hit bottom" and is on its way back up.

New York As Part of a Regional Design

To remain competitive with comparable financial capitals in other countries, Midtown and Lower Manhattan badly need better connections to the airports and to the new, more diffuse, but highly significant concentrations of offices that have grown up in formerly suburban locations in the tri-state metropolitan area. Manhattan is now part of a regional network of business centers, but the transportation system that holds that network together depends heavily on automobiles and is thus subject to enormous inefficiencies. The new Third Regional Plan outlines a relatively economical way of creating a regional rail network by joining and reshaping the existing infrastructure, creating a speedy and efficient alternative to congested highways.

While it is conceivable that some new kind of metropolitan government could coordinate the construction of this rail system, it is more likely that the New York region will have to reshape itself in a continued competitive environment, with fragmented governmental authority divided among three states and their local jurisdictions.

Regional cooperation has already been attained for specific objectives, such as the operations of the Port of New York Authority or the Metropolitan Transportation Administration. Some such mechanism will be needed to create the regional transportation system envisioned in the Third Regional Plan.

Even a better regional transit system would not stop the continued expansion of urbanization around New York City, stimulated by the desire to escape the problems of older areas, and supported by beggar-their-neighbor policies to lure business away from cities. This is a progression that could become a tragedy with profound social, fiscal, and environmental consequences. The United States may have the most dynamic economy in the

world, but no country has the wealth to keep moving the economically successful parts of cities to green-field locations, while writing off existing urban
buildings and infrastructure.

There is a more constructive approach than social warfare, duplicated infrastructure, and continued environmental degradation: the integration of the
new development in former suburbs with New York City, creating a new kind
of metropolitan city, comparable in its way to the metropolis created by the
subways a century earlier.

Ultimately, this transformation requires not only regional transit but
growth boundaries, environmental zoning, and local zoning codes that promote compact communities related to the transportation system. Such actions in turn require state planning legislation, such as exists in Oregon and
Florida. New Jersey has made a beginning on such a plan, and New York and
Connecticut have taken state planning actions in the past. But New York City
doesn't need to wait for regional planning mechanisms to be in place; it can
rebalance the region by transforming its older areas and making them competitive with the suburban fringe.

What New York City needs now is a conceptual strategy, a design that
matches its new realities. New York in the 1950s, and even in its 1969 Master Plan, saw Manhattan south of 60th Street as the metropolitan business
center, supported by bands of industry along the waterfronts, and connected
by subway and bus to its residential neighborhoods. Some of these neighborhoods were slums, but the plans saw them as being restored and improved for their current populations. Beyond New York City were the suburbs, satellites from which commuters, shoppers, theater patrons and
museum-goers traveled into Manhattan.

This earlier pattern still exists; but, as the Third Regional Plan documents,
it is overlaid by a new pattern of almost self-sufficient subregions with their
own business, retail, and cultural centers: in Westchester and Fairfield counties, on Long Island, and in Morris, Somerset, and Middlesex counties in
New Jersey. Meanwhile many of New York's slum neighborhoods and old industrial districts (and similar areas in close-in parts of New Jersey that would
be part of New York City if it were not for the state boundary) have deteriorated to the point that they require total transformation, which opens the
possibility of mixed-income communities instead of low-income ghettos, and
new waterfront districts designed around parks, instead of derelict piers and
deserted factories. Older areas, with their valuable existing infrastructure and
close-to-central locations, could be as desirable as green-field sites on the
suburban fringe. But most people do not yet see the opportunities—only the
problems.

There are at least five ways directly under the city's control by which New York City could redesign itself to be more competitive with suburban areas:

1. Conversion of housing projects into mixed-income communities, with some public housing tenants moving to suburban areas—as in the program recently adopted in Baltimore, or as done at Columbia Point in Boston.

2. Improvements to the public realm (New York can no longer afford its traditional take-it-or-leave-it attitude), including streets, plazas, parks, and public transit.

3. Support for New York's unique functional roles as a business and cultural center. This would include the business improvement districts but could also mean a new focus for the city's educational system, as well as local transportation improvements like the 42nd Street light-rail system.

4. Policies to make now-derelict and deserted areas attractive to new investment, including massive environmental restoration and reclamation. Such policies need design initiatives comparable to those that created Central Park, the redevelopment of Park Avenue north of Grand Central terminal, or Battery Park City. One example of such a plan is the Port Authority's proposal for Hunter's Point.

5. Neighborhood restoration—both physical and social, including neighborhood commercial revitalization—building on initiatives already taken but supported by a much higher level of financial commitment.

Does New York City have the money? A useful first step would be to find out how much money is needed. New York has become so concerned with day-to-day crisis management that very little attention has been given to documenting what the city should do if it could afford to—the essential prerequisite to any increased funding. New York City is in many ways the financial capital of the world. If a proposed policy will ultimately raise property values and tax revenues, there ought to be a way to finance it. The real estate market does not transform derelict industrial areas or remake neighborhoods on its own, but the market could take over and carry these changes out once the newly designed infrastructure and, in some places, consolidation of property ownership are both in place.

The cost of adopting these publicly supported development policies is certainly much less than the future remedial measures that will be necessitated by failure to act now.

New York: A Region at Risk

Robert D. Yaro and Thomas K. Wright

Focused around New York City, the New York–New Jersey–Connecticut Metropolitan Area is the largest urban region in North America and the continent's economic, communications, cultural, and financial hub. During the 19th and 20th centuries this place, which was once a collection of frontier outposts at the edge of a vast, undeveloped continent, became the economic, political, cultural, and communications capital of the world. At the same time it was transformed into a new kind of place, a *metropolitan region*. It has a population of nearly 20 million, a gross regional product of over $600 billion, and a land area of 12,000 square miles. Despite two generations of "decentered" development, half of the region's employment remains in New York City and a dozen regional downtowns, and the region's 1,250-mile rail system carries 40% of the total transit ridership in the country. Since 1970 nearly 3 million immigrants have been admitted to the region—more than one in every five legal admissions to the United States—and two-thirds of them have settled in New York City.

This region is unique in North America not only by its size, strength, and diversity, but also because it spans three states, making attempts to provide region-wide solutions to critical problems much more complex and difficult. Only if the region succeeds in overcoming these complexities, and finds a way to work cooperatively to address the problems it is facing, will it continue to play the role in the 21st century that it has maintained for over 50 years. And as one of the world's first regions to become mature—to begin growing beyond the capacity of its 20th century "modern" infrastructure systems—this region is facing issues that other regions across the globe are either addressing now or will soon have to address.

In the 1920s a visionary group of civic and business leaders came together to consider new ways to deal with daunting problems. Rapid growth was expanding the region beyond long-established political boundaries and the capabilities of existing government institutions. Millions of new residents, many of them poor immigrants from strange and distant places, threatened to overwhelm urban schools and neighborhoods and, some thought, the social fabric as well. New communications technology and industrial institutions were revolutionizing the structure of the economy and the nature of work. And urban sprawl, promoted by widespread automobile ownership and use, was creating uncontrollable traffic congestion and transforming traditional communities and familiar rural landscapes—almost always, it seemed, for the worse.

The Committee on the Regional Plan for New York and its Environs, established 75 years ago and incorporated in 1929 as Regional Plan Association (RPA), was the first organization in the country to try to address these issues with a long-range metropolitan plan. And while particular circumstances have changed, these are still the basic issues that we are dealing with today. The first regional plan provided a compelling new vision for the New York–New Jersey–Connecticut Metropolitan Region, projecting that it would double in population to nearly 20 million by 1965. After the plan was released, the Committee formed RPA, a private nonprofit association, to advocate for the plan's recommendations. During the 1960s, when it became clear that the challenge facing the region was no longer too much urban concentration, but new forces of deconcentration that threatened to hollow out urban centers, RPA prepared its second regional plan. And in February 1996, RPA released the third regional plan, titled *A Region at Risk,* which documents the new set of challenges the region faces and begins a discussion along the lines set out by Jonathan Barnett in the previous case study: providing a strategy that matches the region's new realities and determining how much it will cost to address these regional problems.

This case study outlines RPA's analysis and projections of the New York–New Jersey–Connecticut Metropolitan Region's economy, environment, and social equity—the "Three E's." It summarizes the recommendations of *A Region at Risk* and groups them into five major campaigns that integrate the "Three E's": creating a regional greensward, concentrating growth in centers, improving mobility, investing in a competitive workforce, and reforming governance. Each campaign combines the goals of economic, equity, and environmental improvements, leading the region to a more competitive, prosperous, fair, and sustainable future.

A Summary of the Third Regional Plan

As a new millennium approaches, the metropolitan region of New York, New Jersey, and Connecticut is a region at risk.

- Despite our strength in the global economy, we are facing years of slow growth and uncertainty following our worst recession in 50 years.

- Despite the billions of dollars spent every year by the public and private sectors on infrastructure, office space, and housing, the uncomfortable truth is that we have been living off the legacy of investments of previous generations.

- Despite a history of strength from diversity, a shadow of social division has fallen across the region.

- Despite strict laws and renewed public concern, we continue to pollute our air and water and overrun our rural areas with suburban sprawl.

The region faces a future in which it must compete in a global economy that offers new challenges and opportunities. The question posed is whether the next 25 years will represent the final chapter in a story of prosperity and momentum that dates back to the settlement of Manhattan in the 17th century. The warning is that modest growth in the next few years could mask the beginning of a long, slow, and potentially irreversible and tragic decline.

A regional perspective is the proper scale and context for analyzing and addressing these issues. Metropolitan regions are becoming the dominant economic, environmental, and social actors of the next century. During the 1980s, the metropolitan regions in the United States that grew most rapidly all had central cities that also grew rapidly. And in areas where suburban incomes declined, central cities also experienced decline. Nearly one-third of the income earned in New York City ends up in the pockets of commuters, around $44 billion annually. More than ever, the economies, societies, and environments of all the communities in the Tri-State Metropolitan Region are intertwined, transcending arbitrary political divisions. Our cities and suburbs share a common destiny.

RPA has produced a plan to reconnect the region to its basic foundations, the "Three E's"—economy, environment, and equity—that are the basis of our quality of life (see Figure 1). The fundamental goal of the plan is to rebuild the "Three E's" through investments and policies that integrate and build on our advantages, rather than focusing on just one of the "E's" to the detriment of the others. Currently, economic development is too often border warfare, as states within the region try to steal businesses from each other

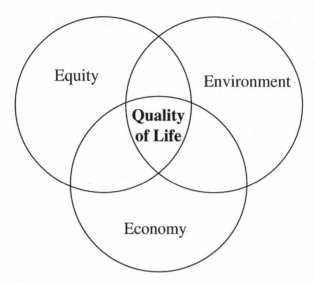

Figure 1. The Three E's.

in what amounts to a zero-sum game. Social issues are either ignored or placated by a vast welfare system that fails to bring people into the economic mainstream. And environmental efforts focus on short-term solutions that attack the symptoms rather than the causes of problems.

Each of these "Three E's" also has broad applicability to metropolitan regions throughout the industrialized world. Virtually every North American metropolitan region, both large and small, faces similar concerns—including shifting employment prospects created by global competition, industry restructuring, and immigration; growing disparities between poorer central cities and inner suburbs and richer outer suburbs; and sprawl and gridlock as a result of decentered, automobile-based growth.

The "Three E's": Where We Are, Where We Are Headed

Economy

Between 1989 and 1992, this region fell into a steep and frightening recession that claimed 770,000 jobs—the largest job loss of any metropolitan area since World War II—eliminating virtually all our growth from the 1980s. Unlike previous recessions, however, all parts of the region suffered losses of similar magnitude. Immediate growth prospects for many key industries remain weak or uncertain, and recovery has been much slower than in other parts of the nation.

This recession and slow recovery must be considered in the context of a wrenching global transformation. New technologies have radically changed how goods and services are produced, marketed, and distributed, and a fiercely competitive global economy can quickly turn the fortunes of a business or a community. Low-skilled workers are particularly vulnerable to this transformation, as automation, rising skill requirements, and corporate downsizing have depressed wages and job opportunities.

But this region has enormous advantages in the emerging global economy. It is the world's most active and innovative center of global capital management, with more than 10,000 international businesses. It is an unsurpassed producer of information, with leadership in broadcasting, book publishing, and magazines and electronic media. This region is a premier designer of popular culture, through the arts, mass marketing, media, and an increasing multiculturalism that equips us to compete directly in dozens of languages and cultures. With over 150 colleges and universities, it is one of the world's largest centers for research and academia. Finally, it is the meeting grounds for governments from around the world, with the United Nations, its affiliates, and permanent missions drawing an unparalleled diversity of people, interests, and ideas.

Over the next decade, the region is likely to experience sluggish growth as employment recovers to its pre-recession peak. Moderate growth fueled by new global markets and information technology will be countered by continued corporate downsizing and global competition. These trends will likely result in continued employment losses in manufacturing and government, but modest increases in financial, business, and personal services.

In the long term, the region has the opportunity to enjoy sustainable economic growth driven by productivity gains and increased sales to expanding global markets (see Figure 2). But that promise could fail without new investments in infrastructure, communities, environment, and the workforce. Increasingly, quality of life is the benchmark against which the region is judged in competition with other regions in the nation and world.

Equity

This region is one of the most diverse in human history. Residents speak more languages, offer a wider array of skills, reside across more extreme densities, and live under the broadest range of incomes in the nation. Demo-

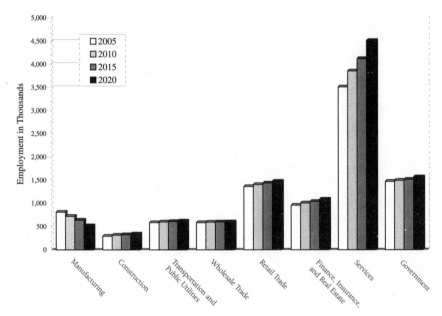

Figure 2. Projected Employment, 2005 to 2020. *Source:* New York Metropolitan Transportation Council.

graphic projections show that it will be even more diverse in the future (see Figure 3). By the year 2020 a majority of the region's residents will be of African, Asian, or Hispanic heritage, largely as a result of a constant flow of immigrants from around the globe. Since 1970 the region has drawn nearly 3 million legal immigrants, almost one-fifth of the nation's total legal entries. Throughout the 1990s and beyond, immigrants and their children will account for virtually all of the region's expansion in working-age population. These new residents bring with them enormous talent and cultural diversity—New York City could never have become the world capital it is without them.

But even as we become a more diverse society, disturbing trends show that we are becoming a more isolated and fragmented society. Low-skilled workers face a future of declining incomes and sporadic employment, and over 2 million residents of the region already live in poverty. Nearly 3 million adults in the region are estimated to be functionally illiterate. Most new jobs will demand at least some college or post-secondary education, yet a large share of urban students never finish high school. And poverty remains much more concentrated among nonwhite residents, even when differences in education

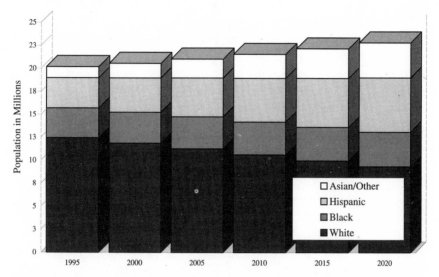

Figure 3. Projected Population, 1995 to 2020. *Source:* New York Metropolitan
Transportation Council.

and skills are accounted for, demonstrating that bias and segregation remain
persistent problems.

Entire communities are being left out of the region's growing prosperity, as
too many people have come to accept the concept of a permanent underclass.
Some people now see our diversity not as the enormous advantage it provides in the world economy, but as a hindrance. For a prosperous future, this
region must do a better job of welcoming and assimilating its present immigrant population, as well as the 1.25 million new immigrants expected in the
next 10 years. Isolated by physical barriers—such as a lack of housing or
public transportation alternatives—that separate residences from new employment opportunities, inner-city communities have been cut off from the
new employment centers in the region's suburbs. The region needs to work
harder to integrate isolated and racially diverse communities into its social
fabric and economic mainstream.

These communities can either be an enormous advantage, or a liability, depending on the policies put in place now, from affordable housing to education to economic development.

Environment

This region is a national leader in environmental protection, having enacted
comprehensive and far-reaching environmental standards and having spent

the money and political capital needed to make the laws work. As a result, the region has added 350,000 acres of public parkland since the 1960s, while air and water quality have improved significantly. Yet these achievements can obscure the serious nature of the problems that still confront us. Most of the region does not meet federal air quality standards. More and more drinking water must now be filtered. Many urban neighborhoods lack park acreage, and suburban development continues to sprawl across mountains and farmland.

In the past 30 years a new pattern of land use has swept the region, involving the construction of massive campus-style commercial and industrial facilities in sprawling residential suburbs. From 1970 to 1995, core urban counties lost more than 300,000 jobs, while the outer suburban ring gained 2 million. Eighty percent of the 1.7 million housing units built since 1970 were constructed in the region's outer ring, as residents sought affordable housing, lower taxes, and an escape from the problems of cities and inner suburbs. But these rings of deconcentrated suburbs consume vast areas of open land and shatter traditional patterns of community.

The spread-out pattern of homes and jobs has led people to drive more than ever. The number of vehicle miles traveled in the region grew by 60% from 1970 to 1990, creating congestion on highways and roads. Growing use of automobiles, trucks, and buses is also the key reason why the region is second only to Los Angeles in number of days that air quality fails to meet federal standards. But current toll policies are absolutely backward, rejecting the fundamental market principle of charging more for a scarce resource. Instead, tolls are discounted for commuters who use the roads during the most crowded times. Furthermore, free parking is often provided and gasoline is now cheaper in constant dollars than it has ever been, costing less than bottled water.

At the same time the region has abandoned urban areas, hollowing out cities that historically have been the locus for jobs and residences. By 1980 the majority of the region's residents did not live in a city. The most visible impact of this has been the conversion of forests, farms, and wetlands to urban uses and the paving of wildlife habitat and natural resources. The region lost 40% of its farmland between 1964 and 1987, and development outside urban areas continues at around 30,000 acres per year.

This challenge comes at a time of widespread dissatisfaction with environmental management by business and the public sectors. Government policies that call for polluted sites to be cleaned by their owners often impede beneficial site restoration. In 1994 more than $4.6 billion in state, federal, and local funds were allocated for water pollution control in coastal waters, and $2.8 billion was spent disposing of garbage. But all of the region's landfills will reach capacity around the year 2000, and we will be spending more on pollution control and disposal in the future.

Efforts to protect the environment from further degradation will have to begin by looking at the causes of problems—such as land use and transportation—to find innovative and comprehensive solutions. We can do a better job of protecting the environment and living within our means by learning to produce less waste, recycle, and rely on biological systems for natural resource management and pollution control.

The Five Campaigns

Strategies for improving the region's quality of life must reinforce all three of the cornerstone E's and demonstrate how our economy, equity, and environment are vitally linked to each other, or those strategies may be counterproductive.

Five initiatives anchor the plan—*Greensward, Centers, Mobility, Workforce,* and *Governance*. Each campaign addresses all three E's. Together, they have been designed to reenergize the region by regreening, reconnecting, and re-centering it. The *Greensward* safeguards the region's green infrastructure of forests, watersheds, estuaries, and farms, and it establishes green limits for future growth. *Centers* focuses the next generation of growth in the region's existing downtown employment and residential areas. *Mobility* creates a new transportation network that knits together the restrengthened centers. *Workforce* provides groups and individuals living in these centers with the skills and connections needed to bring them into the economic mainstream. Achieving these ends will require new ways of organizing and energizing our political and civic institutions, as outlined in *Governance*. Collectively, all of these strategies underpin the region's quality of life and can guide us to sustainable growth as we enter the 21st century.

The goal of the campaigns in the Third Regional Plan is to integrate and improve the region's economy, environment, and equity, thereby improving our quality of life (see Figure 4).

Greensward

Two generations of decentralized growth have drastically increased the region's urban land—by 60% in 30 years despite only a 13% increase in pop-

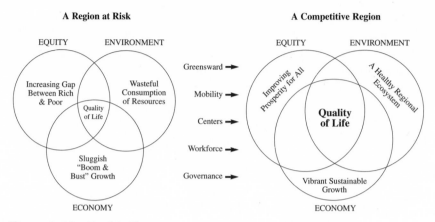

Figure 4. The Graphic Plan.

ulation (see Figure 5). Continuing exurban development at a rate of more than 30,000 acres per year threatens large areas of open land and critical environmental resources at the region's outer edge, more than 50 miles from Manhattan.

The region needs a greensward that safeguards water and food supplies as well as recreational opportunities and shapes future growth by integrating protected large-scale landscape resources, an established regional network of greenways, and revitalized urban parks and open spaces. The greensward makes economic sense, protecting the environmental infrastructure that would otherwise require costly cleanup and pollution controls. It will provide important benefits to people, safeguarding access to recreation and natural and agricultural landscapes. And it will be good for the environment, providing a long-term and comprehensive plan to reconcile local land use and development with broader regional objectives.

RPA is undertaking projects designed to protect key open space tracts, manage natural resources, protect productive farmland, provide land use planning assistance to local communities, and revitalize urban parks. Eleven landscapes and coastal estuaries are of particular concern: the Long Island Pine Barrens and Peconic Estuary; Catskill Mountains; Shawangunk and Kittatinny mountains; New York–New Jersey–Connecticut Appalachian Highlands; Hudson River; Delaware River; New Jersey Pinelands; Long Island Sound; New York/New Jersey Harbor; Atlantic seashore; and disappearing

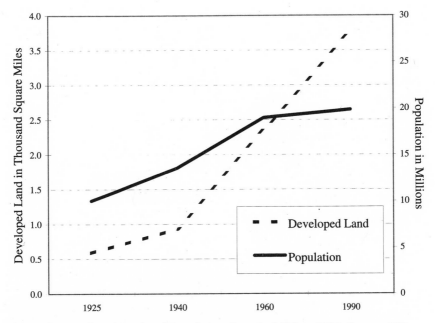

Figure 5. Developed Land and Population Growth, 1925 to 1990. *Sources:* RPA and U.S. Census Bureau.

active farmland (see Figure 6). These reserves comprise 2.5 million acres that are currently at risk of being consumed by sprawl. Models for protection of these areas already exist in the New Jersey Pinelands and especially in the Long Island Pine Barrens, where a new locally controlled commission is protecting 50,000 acres and supervising development on another 50,000 acres. The recent agreement between New York City and upstate communities to balance growth and protection of the watershed builds on this experience.

Major recommendations of the *Greensward* campaign include:

- Establish 11 regional reserves in the areas listed above to protect public water supplies, estuaries, natural habitats, and farmlands and to function as an urban growth boundary for the region.

- Reinvest in urban parks, public spaces, and natural resources, restoring and creating new spaces in urban neighborhoods and along waterfronts.

- Create a regional network of greenways to provide access to recreational areas.

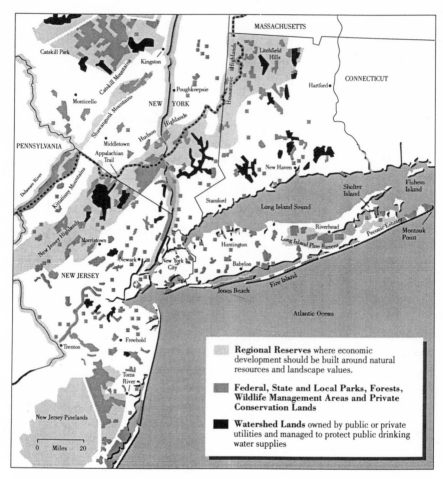

Figure 6. The Regional Greensward.

Centers

Recent development patterns have shifted resources and investment away from the region's cities and inner suburbs so that virtually all our employment growth in the past 30 years has been in areas located outside existing centers. Unless this trend is reversed, the region will face ever-worsening problems of limited access to employment opportunities, wide income disparities, social isolation, environmental degradation, and lack of affordable housing. Already, economic consequences of decayed cities, traffic congestion, and the region's deteriorating quality of life are apparent.

The region must work to improve quality of life and economic opportunities in centers, including not only the region's Central Business District but also downtowns throughout the region, such as Newark, Poughkeepsie, and Bridgeport. Centers provide a more efficient use of resources and reduce costs for the entire regional economy. Centers also reduce land consumption and allow us to conserve a greater portion of our remaining open space. And because these areas are more accessible to less-advantaged communities, investing in and bringing new employment to centers brings new opportunities to the residents who need them most.

In the 1960s RPA's Second Regional Plan pointed out the damaging character of the emerging suburban patterns of retail strips and malls, office parks, and large lot subdivisions, and it warned against abandoning older urban communities. But these admonitions went largely unheeded here and nearly everywhere else in metropolitan America, as we built a new civilization around the interstate highways and moved away from cities and older suburban neighborhoods. Communities encouraged growth to expand their tax rolls, but they now face rising demand for services and infrastructure and revolts from hard-pressed taxpayers. High housing prices, exacerbated by rising land values, command a larger share of everyone's resources. Residents who now live with congestion and sky-high tax bills and mortgage payments find their lives to be less convenient, less safe, or less connected to their communities. Growing numbers of the region's residents have sought refuge by moving even farther out into the suburbs and exurbs, threatening to repeat these patterns in outer rings of the region. Many residents have chosen to leave the region altogether, in search of greater quality of life and economic opportunity.

In response to these trends, a number of architects, landscape architects, urban designers, and planners have come together under the banner of the Congress for the New Urbanism (CNU). CNU has begun to promote alternative models for suburban growth, generally based on the concept of building new, planned, compact, mixed-use village and town centers. Many of these new town plans are based on older models of town planning—including the work of early 20th century planners from the Garden City Movement, including Raymond Unwin, Frederick Law Olmsted, Jr., and John Nolen— that were first promoted in this country by RPA's 1929 Regional Plan. These trends have formed an important movement in planning and architecture, and they have improved the design of new communities and brought historical contextualism back into urban design.

But the tri-state region is mature. It does not require the development of a significant number of new towns. Our built environment consists of hundreds of traditional towns, villages, and hamlets, many with access to the regional rail system and with room for significant infill and expansion. RPA seeks more to refocus development and investment in existing centers than to create new development at the region's edge. Our traditional centers are still located in the region's core, the form of which has been altered from uniform concentric rings of development to a pattern in which each subregion has developed connections to the core along suburban corridors. Robert Geddes has suggested the analogy of each subregion being the petal of a rose, each with its own life-supporting connection to the center (see Figure 7). The recommendations in the plan are designed to reinforce these connections, both between the petals and the core and among the petals themselves.

These goals will only be realized through an aggressive campaign to improve downtowns, from reconfiguring transit connections, to rethinking

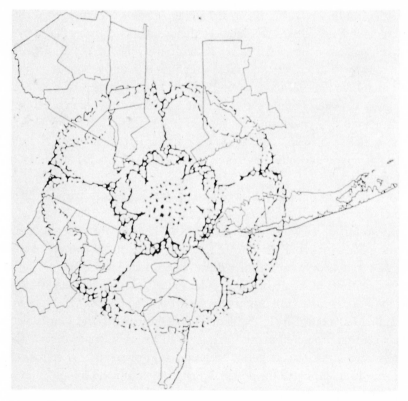

Figure 7. The Tri-State Region as a Rose.

urban design, to establishing new job opportunities. The *Centers* campaign will direct as much job growth as possible to central business districts in the region's major downtowns and encourage residential growth in a constellation of centers. The goal is to maintain the approximately 50% share that centers currently have of the region's employment. To do this, the campaign will work for new public–private investments, creative planning and zoning, and expansion of arts and cultural activities that foster the kind of desirable mixed-use communities that will attract jobs and residents to centers.

Most successful centers evolve over generations, eventually forming a network of established communities. The challenge here, and in other metropolitan regions that developed around rail systems, is to revitalize, rebuild, round-out, and gradually infill the existing constellation of town centers. But where suburban sprawl already exists, or where brownfields are being reclaimed, the principles of the new urbanism could be applied to create new centers, retrofitting density onto sprawl. And in some greensward areas small, well-sited new communities could also be designed around these principles.

Major recommendations of the *Centers* campaign include:

- Strengthen the region's Central Business District by building a Crosstown light-rail system and district, expanding transit access to Lower Manhattan and the Jersey City waterfront, and revitalizing downtown Brooklyn and Long Island City.

- Invest in 11 regional downtowns—New Haven, Bridgeport, Stamford, White Plains, Poughkeepsie, Hicksville, Mineola, Jamaica, Newark, New Brunswick, and Trenton—attracting new job growth and rebuilding communities rather than building on greenfield sites.

- Create incentives for new development and investment in transit- and pedestrian-friendly centers throughout the region, so that they provide the quality of life that makes living and working in centers worthwhile.

- Support new institutions and uses in centers, such as "telematic" at-home businesses, mixed-use districts, and arts and cultural institutions.

Mobility

Mobility throughout the region is hampered by limited and fragmented transit service, a freight rail system that terminates at the west side of the Hudson River, and congested and bottlenecked roads. There is little capacity for growth on the current highway system, unless new development takes place even further from the center of the region. At the same time, the public transportation system requires new commitment and investment simply to maintain it in a state of good repair.

The region should invest in a Regional Express Rail (*Rx*) network to bring mobility throughout the region to world-class standards (see Figure 8). This can be accomplished with only 25 miles of new rail track—a 2% expansion of the existing system—and by reusing abandoned or under-utilized infrastructure. Improved mobility would strengthen the region's economy by reducing travel times and transfers to employment centers and airports, improving freight connections, and using the road system more efficiently with less congestion. It would improve our society, as less-advantaged communities become better connected to employment opportunities. And regional mobility would improve our environment, allowing people and goods to travel more quickly and thus with less pollution.

The *Mobility* campaign has three principal components: improved transit service, a transformed freight system, and a highway network with reduced congestion. The campaign will promote the *Rx* network to support the centers of commerce and provide fuller access to major employment sites. RPA will advance strategies that promote a more efficient system of freight movement in the region. And the campaign will work to institute market-based transportation pricing measures that recognize the full public and private costs of transportation and that add efficiency through market incentives.

Major recommendations of the *Mobility* campaign include:

- Construct the *Rx* system to provide: (1) airport access by connecting the Long Island Railroad to Grand Central Terminal, Lower Manhattan, Kennedy Airport, and LaGuardia Airport; (2) direct access from New Jersey and Long Island to the East Side and Lower Manhattan; (3) direct service from the Hudson Valley and Connecticut to the West Side and Lower Manhattan; (4) through service from New Jersey to Connecticut and Long Island; and (5) service between the boroughs in a new circumferential subway line.

- Promote congestion-busting through road-pricing and market approaches such as tolls and employer incentives. Also, complete the missing links in the highway network that support existing centers or remedy notorious bottlenecks.

- Improve commercial transportation by building a trans-Hudson freight rail crossing, thus cutting congestion on the highway system.

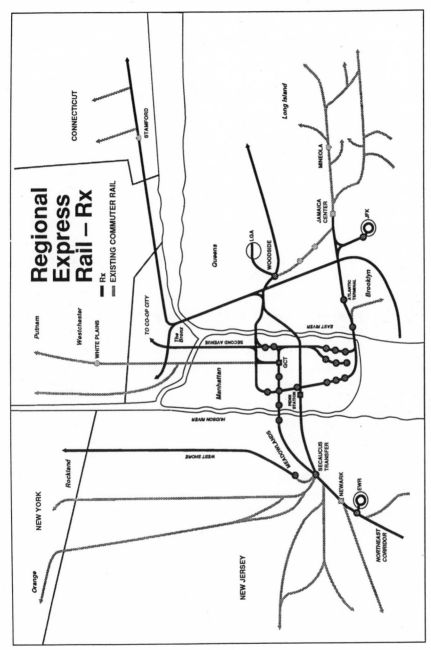

Figure 8. Regional Express Rail—Rx.

Workforce

The emerging economy in today's global market will require a competitive, educated workforce to perform increasingly complex jobs. High-paying jobs in growing international service industries will be particularly demanding of new skills. But entire communities are being left behind by these trends, failed by the institutions and regulations that should allow them to become full participants in a growing economy.

The region must help provide young people and adults, particularly from low-income communities, with the skills and access needed to participate in information- and technology-based industries. Workforce development ensures economic growth by supplying the workers needed for new technology-based activities and by increasing productivity. It addresses social equity by closing the skill gap that creates larger disparities in income. And it improves our environment by focusing growth into urban centers, rather than encouraging more businesses to move out to the suburbs.

RPA calls upon the region's business, education, labor, and civic institutions both to develop a system of lifelong learning that meets the requirements of a competitive, knowledge-based economy and to reform institutions and regulations to allow low-income communities to participate fully in the mainstream economy. The campaign will identify existing strengths and weaknesses in our current systems and propose benchmarks for regional institutions. RPA will also support increased private-sector participation in workforce development initiatives and will advocate policies to increase school financing in low-income communities, encourage greater participation by immigrant populations in the mainstream economy, loosen restrictions on "informal" economic activities, and improve access to information, telecommunications, and transportation services for poorer communities.

Major recommendations of the *Workforce* campaign include:

- Improve education in low-income communities by combining state financing of public education with local management reforms and teaching innovations.
- Reconnect education and the workplace with local school-to-work alliances linking schools to employers; develop state tax incentives to encourage continuous education for adult workers; and create a tri-state council of business, labor, education, and civic leaders to coordinate workforce development initiatives.
- Bring immigrants and minorities into the mainstream economy by expand-

ing English literacy programs, legitimizing informal economic activities, and seeking moderate reform of federal immigration statutes.

- Connect low-income communities by expanding support for community-based organizations, improving transportation links to job centers, and using new information technologies to expand job information networks.

Governance

The region is composed of 20 million people living in 13,000 square miles governed by over 2,000 units of government, including counties, cities, towns, service districts, and authorities. Each of these political entities is funded almost exclusively through property tax, and the majority of them control their own independent budgets. The result is fiscal imbalance and inefficiencies in the form of duplication of efforts, depletion and degradation of natural resources, self-serving and shortsighted decisions, cumbersome land use regulatory processes, and inadequate delivery of public services.

The *Governance* campaign will refocus state government and regional authorities, enabling us to build and manage world-class infrastructure and reduce regulatory burdens and tax inefficiencies. The reform of governance is necessary for the region's economy, as it is clear that we cannot support current deficient systems with delays and expensive regulations. Governance is critical to providing greater equity for the region's society, in public education, land use, and service delivery. And governance is crucial to protecting our environment as we reform land use regulations that currently encourage sprawl rather than redevelopment.

Through reform of taxation and land use regulations, RPA will promote faster and better delivery of public services with less duplication, fewer layers of bureaucracy, and a reduction in conflicting mandates. The *Governance* campaign will propose more efficient public capital infrastructure investments, as identified in the plan, as well as effective state development plans and growth boundaries.

Major recommendations of the *Governance* campaign include:

- Coordinate governance in the region through state growth management plans, education finance reform, service sharing, and new regional coalitions, such as: (1) an annual "G-3" governors' conference to coordinate policies and investments to promote regional competitiveness and a regional compact between the three governors to reduce border-warfare economic development policies; (2) a Tri-State Congressional Coalition to fight for essential federal tax and regulatory reforms and infrastructure funds; a Tri-State Business Council composed of the major regional chambers of commerce and partnerships to coordinate regional promotion and advocacy and develop a regional business plan.

- Create new public institutions to finance and provide regional services, such as a Tri-State Regional Transportation Authority, a restructured Port Authority, and a Tri-State Infrastructure Bank.

- Improve public and private decision-making processes, incorporating sustainable economics in accounting and tax and regulatory systems and utilizing smart infrastructure approaches to capital investments.

Paying for the Plan

If fully implemented, the plan's five campaigns will yield a range of benefits that include stronger and more sustainable economic growth, a more cohesive society with a more equitable distribution of prosperity, cleaner air and water, less congestion, more attractive communities, and a rich legacy for future generations. Many of these benefits cannot be quantified because we lack the tools to measure them effectively. However, a plausible scenario can be constructed to demonstrate the difference between current trends and the result of a proactive strategy to reinvest in the region's human, physical, and natural resources.

For the past several decades the region's share of the national economy has declined. If this trend continues at the same rate, the region will decline from around 9% of the national gross domestic product today to about 7% by 2020. Figure 9 shows two projections for our gross regional product—continuing its declining share of the nation's GDP (scenario 1) or maintaining its current share and growing at the same rate as the rest of the country (scenario 2). The chart shows that holding our share of the nation's growth could translate into an additional $200 billion annually in the region's economy by 2020.

The investments, policies, and governance reforms recommended in the plan do not guarantee that the region will achieve this goal. In fact, in the short run the region will probably continue to see some decline in its share of national GDP. But long-term paybacks from the investments proposed in the plan could make it possible for the region to stabilize its share within the next decade. This strategy would be supported by the region's expanding links to global markets that are expected to grow more rapidly than the U.S.

Scenario	1995	2000	2005	2010	2015	2020
1. Continued Decline in National Share	$640	$690	$730	$760	$780	$800
2. Stabilized Share of National Growth	$640	$700	$760	$830	$900	$1,010
Difference	*$0*	*$10*	*$30*	*$70*	*$120*	*$210*

Notes:

Scenario 1 assumes that the region's share of the gross domestic product declines at the same rate that it did in the 1975 to 1995 period.

Scenario 2 assumes that investments in education, infrastructure, and the environment, as well as government reforms, generate sufficient growth to stabilize the region's share of national growth.

Figure 9. Projected Gross Regional Product (in billions of 1994 dollars), 1995 to 2020.

economy. The sooner we begin investing in these resources, the sooner we will gain the benefits of them.

To implement the recommendations in three campaigns—*Greensward, Centers,* and *Mobility*—RPA estimates that the region will need to invest $75 billion above current spending levels in capital expenditures over the next 25 years. Specifically, the plan estimates that establishing the 11 regional reserves, instituting greenways, and cleaning up urban parks and waterfronts will cost $11 billion; that $17 billion will be necessary to attract new jobs and development to the region's downtowns and to make significant progress in affordable housing needs; and that building a world-class express rail system while improving highway and freight movement will cost $47 billion. The recommendations of the *Workforce* campaign carry additional costs—from returning public schools to a state of good repair to addressing adult literacy—that are more difficult to estimate.

RPA proposes that these investments be funded through a combination of strategies that increase government efficiency or charge users for services, rather than increasing general taxes. Even with recent downsizing in state and local government, innovative approaches to right-sizing government and the reduced costs of providing services to compact centers can achieve additional savings of several billion dollars. Phasing out costly "border-warfare" economic development strategies would also provide significant revenue for investment—as much as $500 million annually if tax incentives to businesses were reduced by half. Major new revenue sources could include incentive-based tolls on highways and bridges, a 1-cent charge per vehicle mile traveled, and a 10-cent per gallon tax on gasoline. These fees could yield a total of $40 billion over the next 25 years. To pay for watershed protection and open space preservation, new development fees, a property tax surcharge in the regional reserves, and a 0.001-cent charge per gallon of water could generate over $300 million a year. Finally, the plan's investments would yield additional revenue from stronger economic growth. An increase in gross regional product of $200 billion by 2020 could produce an additional $20 billion annually in state and municipal tax collection, even with a decrease in tax rates.

When combined, these revenue sources could provide financing for the $75 billion in infrastructure investments as well as many of the *Workforce* investments proposed in the plan.

Call to Action

Regional Plan Association has prepared an ambitious plan that targets new investments necessary for sustained growth and continued prosperity in an uncertain future. The plan calls for radical changes in the status quo and bold initiative on the part of citizens. Some of the recommendations carry significant price tags, but the Tri-State Metropolitan Region cannot afford *not* to make these investments. Projections and analysis demonstrate that we are reaching the end of credible short-term solutions and must begin to look at the fundamental causes of our mounting problems. At their root, these issues are all regional and will require comprehensive approaches for meaningful improvements.

The five campaigns outlined in this document are presented in greater detail in *A Region at Risk: The Third Regional Plan for the New York–New Jersey–Connecticut Metropolitan Area* (Island Press, 1996). To succeed, each campaign will need the active support and cooperation of government, business, and civic leadership. To the degree that our elected officials do not provide the necessary leadership, we must form new civic coalitions to demand change. These new "third-sector" coalitions will build on one of the region's untapped strengths—its thousands of community, business, environmental, and other groups. New coalitions are already being formed that bring together competing interests and forge new ways of addressing old problems. These include coalitions between environmentalists and developers, between government and business, and between local interests and regional imperatives. By looking at the long term and considering the interlocking goals of economy, equity, and environment, we can build on our strengths and enter the next millennium strategically placed for another century of growth and prosperity. But we must act now. The region's competitiveness and sustainability in a changing world hang in the balance.

Cascadia: Portland, Seattle, and Vancouver

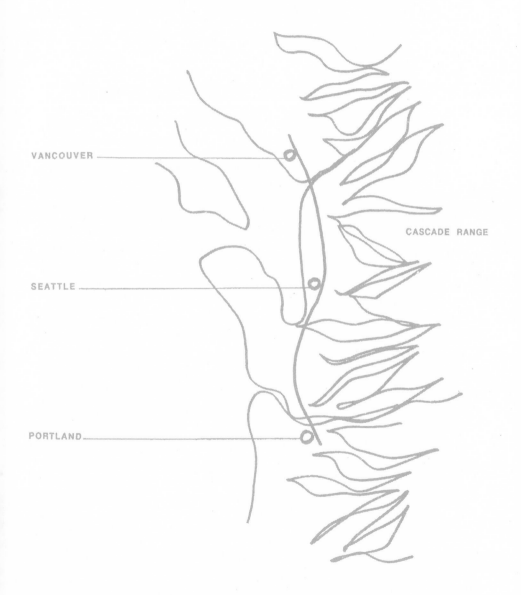

VANCOUVER

SEATTLE

PORTLAND

CASCADE RANGE

Cascadia is an emerging concept of a city-region. The case study of Cascadia is written by urbanists from its three major cities, Portland (Ethan Seltzer, a regional land use planner), Seattle (Anne Vernez Moudon, an urban designer), and Vancouver (Alan Artibise, an urban program consultant). Each portrays the growth and form of their city, and collaboratively they set forth the possibilities of a new city-region.

Cascadia is unique, insofar as it takes its name and its form from *nature*— the Cascade mountain range that parallels the Pacific coastline. As it winds its way through the political boundaries of two nations, "Cascadia can be said to share a common culture rooted in the landscape of the Northwest." But, Cascadia is not unique, in the sense that the equilibrium of nature and culture is the essence of city building.

Cascadia is both an *economic* idea, integrating the emerging settlements along a regional corridor (a "main street" called Interstate 5), and an *ecological* idea, informed by the geology, vegetation, natural species, climate ("the rain coast"), and movement of water in and through the settlements.

The three cities have pioneered in planning for environmental protection and the provision of "greenspace" (parks, riparian corridors, and natural habitats) as parts of the urban fabric. Today, however, their well-being is at risk. The greatest challenge comes from the high rate of population growth; moreover, the pattern of human settlement is consuming land at a much faster rate than the rate of population growth. Sprawl development has caused inefficient use of land, energy, and other resources. More people, more cars, and more settlement have profound impacts on the air quality, the

147

hydrology of watersheds, and the environmental health of the inhabitants. The question raised by the notion of Cascadia is, "will the legacy of our times result in the stewardship of the environment, or the destructive consumption of one of the most striking and abundant landscapes on the continent?"

The three cities have made strong commitments to social equity. Embodied in their urban form strategies, such as growth boundaries, compact developments, "complete communities," and mixed-use "urban villages," are intentions to meet fairly the needs of a broad, diverse group of residents. Cascadia is an idea based on an ideal of social justice: "the hardest task, and the most urgent, will be to create a culture of inhabitation that reflects not only a vision of place, but a vision of society."

Like Manchester in the 19th century, and New York and Los Angeles in the 20th century, Cascadia may be the "shock city" of the 21st century. But, it will not be shocking in the old ways.

Cascadia: An Emerging Regional Model

Alan Artibise, Anne Vernez Moudon, and Ethan Seltzer

In this era of metropolitan "citistates," cities are reassessing and redefining their interests in both global and local terms. Gone are the days when cities could unilaterally pursue their interests, believing, perhaps naively, that their boundaries described discrete territories of concern. Perhaps nowhere in North America is this new local–global construct quite so seductive as in the Pacific Northwest. The idea of "Cascadia" has captured the imagination of policymakers and citizens alike and has already spawned a wide range of planning initiatives and new institutional arrangements.

There is good reason for this sense of excitement and optimism. Cascadia encompasses, by most definitions, some of the most beautiful scenery and productive ecologies of North America. To a large degree, despite the intervention of international and other jurisdictional boundaries, Cascadia can be said to share a common culture rooted in the landscape of the Northwest. Close to 75% of the population of Oregon, Washington, and British Columbia can be found in its three principal cities, Portland, Seattle, and Vancouver, B.C., each of which in turn has received recognition for its high quality of urban life and design. If the economies of Oregon, Washington, and British Columbia were joined, the result would represent one of the largest economies in the world, and a diversified one at that. Finally, Cascadia is strategically positioned on the Pacific Rim and, in fact, is geographically closer to major Asian markets than any other metropolitan region in North America.

Cascadia is today more of an idea than a reality. Actually defining the boundaries for Cascadia elicits different responses from different actors. To some, the power of the idea rests in its utility as a vehicle for reorganizing our inhabitation of the Pacific Northwest along bioregional lines. To others, the economic power represented along Cascadia's "main street," Interstate 5 and Highway 99, suggests opportunities that carry over well into the next century. Finally, to a growing number of people, the possibility of merging the bioregional view with the economic view into a truly sustainable vision for human inhabitation of a region is exciting and compelling.

Whatever the case, the idea of Cascadia is changing the view that Northwesterners have of their region, their respective cities, and their role in a global environment (see Figure 1). The notion of Cascadia is a force for cultural change in the Northwest, possibly along lines that will enable the region to remain a highly desirable and pleasurable place to live. Initial steps toward

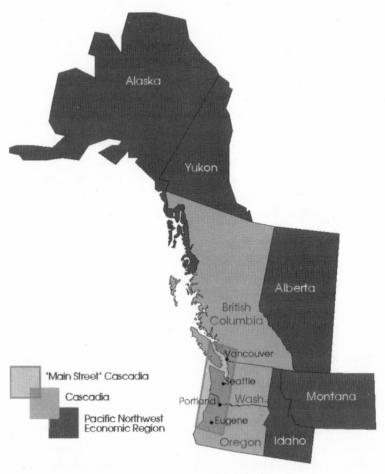

Figure 1. Cascadia's Place in the Pacific Northwest.

forging the Cascadian alliance—promoting the "two nation vacation," developing a bid for hosting the Olympics, creating new links among colleges and universities, smoothing the way for the 23 million annual international border crossings, and even creating a Cascadian flag and "Visa" card, to name a few—are slowly bearing fruit and advancing our understanding of what putting the idea into practice might mean.

Metropolitan Portland

Metropolitan Portland has been receiving a lot of attention recently. The metropolitan area and the city of Portland have been lauded as examples of what seems to be working, or at least holds promise for working, in urban areas in the future. The issue, of course, is the emptying out of cities into sprawling metropolitan areas, accompanied by devastating impacts on environmental quality and community cohesion. Although the Portland metropolitan area has not met and slain all the dragons of this particular story, it has managed to avoid some things and to do others right—right enough to garner national and international attention.

However, it was less than 60 years ago, in 1938, when Lewis Mumford visited our region at the invitation of the Northwest Regional Council, a group drawn from Washington, Oregon, Idaho, and Montana to coordinate the efforts of "agencies concerned with the orderly development of the Pacific Northwest." Mumford had this to say about Portland:

> . . . neither Portland nor Seattle show, from the standpoint of planning, more than metropolitan ambitions that have over-reached themselves. The melancholy plan to increase Portland's population from 300,000 to three million succeeded in disordering and unfocussing its growth: but it did little to give it the benefit of modern city planning practice; meanwhile, the apparent financial prospects of these port cities undermined the base of the sounder development that could well have been taking place in other parts of the region, on strictly modern lines.

Though much has been achieved since Mumford's gloomy assessment, observers today should condition what they see with the following: First, there are no silver bullets or supremely right answers. It takes a mix of many interrelated and complementary actions to be successful. Second, you must make your own successes wherever you find yourself. Use our experience as a reminder that much, truly, is possible. Third, recognize that metropolitan

Portland is not "done" yet. Issues of education, social equity, and public safety wait for thorough treatment. Much has been done, but much remains to be attended to.

There are six main drivers for the physical and policy environment for the Portland region today. They are discussed in the following sections.

The Landscape

Today, prior to settlement by whites, and for some 10,000 years of Native American settlement, this has been an incredibly beautiful and abundant landscape. The seasonal cycle of the native peoples brought new sources of sustenance by the month. The salmon trade extended from Canada to California, and east over the Rocky Mountains. The broad plains of the Willamette Valley, south and west of Portland, were managed through burning to concentrate wildlife in "tree islands" and to make digging of the camas root easier.

To the early settlers, this was promoted as an Eden, a garden, and it was! Through disease, the native cultures were decimated by the early 1840s, some 10,000 years of cultural evolution and adaptation wiped out in the space of about 5 years. Settlers arriving over the Oregon Trail, a six-month journey, discovered a landscape that very much looked like a garden and was virtually empty. Of course, believing that this Eden had been prepared specifically for them, they began to inhabit the landscape in the image of the lands they had left behind. The view was most often outward, with early settlement backed up against the woods with a view out across the valley floor and to the surrounding mountains. The landscape was and is inspiring, overpowering the works of man as many historians of the West have noted.

Today, that connection to nature, and willingness to elevate environment to a pressing concern, is still central to the policy debates surrounding growth management and the future of our cities. Note, too, that this presents an incredible challenge, since there is very little of an urban nature that has been found to improve on Eden. Hence, although environment is an important and central value, we have yet to express a truly urban vision for this corner of the West.

Agrarian Settlement

From about 1830 until 1880, the settlement of the Portland metropolitan area was accomplished by farmers arriving from the border states of the Midwest. Simply put, they came for health and wealth, and found themselves in a land of rich soils and forgiving climate. The challenge here has not been to get things to grow but to cut them back fast enough. Consequently, our parcels are small but productive.

Our cities emerged as service centers to the farming economy of the territory south of the Columbia River. Oregon became a state in 1859, some 30 years before Washington. By the time the major waves of industrialization hit our shores, our cities were established along different lines with different sets of interests.

Speculative City Building

From about 1850 until World War II, the Oregon story was one of speculative city building with ever-widening settlement based on the available transportation technology. Early Portland was simply referred to as "the Clearing," a wide spot on the way between the fertile Tualatin Valley to the west and the territorial seat in Oregon City to the south.

From the start, Portland was in heated competition with settlements along the Willamette and Columbia rivers for the designation as the "head" of navigation. Because of its position along the Willamette River, downstream of the most treacherous sand bars, and its location at the gateway to the Tualatin Valley, Portland won out. From the start, with its original plat in the 1850s, Portland's early speculators and boosters believed that they were building what would one day be a great city. They set aside a strip of "park blocks" running the length of the city at a time when the total population was only several hundred and there were more stumps than people in evidence.

Downtown Portland inherited its 200-foot by 200-foot blocks from the decisions made by these same folks to maximize the rent received from higher priced corner lots. The smaller the blocks, the more corners to rent per land claim. The small lots also aided flood drainage by providing more "channels" back to the river itself.

The city began its growth close to the river, but spread inland and across the river as trails became roads, street trolleys and railroads widened the ring, and bridges were built to replace ferries. In fact, roads were so bad prior to World War II that Portland's interurban rail system was reputed to be the third largest in the nation by early in this century. In 1924 Portland adopted zoning after a series of defeats at the polls. The primary thrust of that initiative had to do with maintaining the exclusivity of residential and largely segregated neighborhoods.

Today, the legacy of small lots has left us with a walkable, pedestrian-scale downtown, and the park blocks form the core of a regional attraction. Our streetcar suburbs retain their value, enjoying a new life in this era of new urbanism. The blatant and, by the standards of today, outrageous segregation of then suburban neighborhoods has given way to the economic segregation within subdivision walls so common across our current metropolitan landscapes.

The Car

From the late 1930s to the present, this region like every other in North America has been under the spell of the automobile. When the car was added to the settlement pattern of earlier years, the basic matrix didn't change. Grid systems of streets and neighborhoods interspersed with commercial activity, parks, and public places were and remain typical in these older parts of the region. However, in the post-war region we have experienced the same pattern of strictly separated uses, underprovision of public space and parks, and overloading of old, radial farm-to-market roads and highways that others have. The settlement pattern of the region reflects these trends, although neither our rate of growth or extent of suburbanization can match that of other western metropolitan areas.

Downtown Reinvestment

The 1950s were an interesting time for us. In the mid-1950s, Lloyd Center, a pioneer shopping mall, opened in an inner-eastside neighborhood, just across the river from downtown, with 600,000 people living within 20 minutes travel. In 1958 downtown business leaders, alarmed at the weakening of downtown's historic retail focus, worked with the city of Portland to form the Portland Development Commission (PDC). The PDC initiated urban renewal and "slum clearance" measures in what is now south downtown, removing Portland's Jewish and Italian communities from the downtown scene.

Perhaps most important in PDC's activities was the development of a vital public–private partnership that resulted in the downtown plan of the early 1970s. The downtown plan was funded by both the business community and the city, and it resulted in projects ranging from the transit mall to pedestrian improvements associated with every new building.

Public Policy and Land Use Planning

In the mid-1960s what was left of the garden-like landscape of the Willamette Valley was threatened by sprawl. The Willamette River itself was an unfortunate example of an unfishable, unswimmable stream, and productive farms were passing into various forms of urban development. Resource exploitation had been central to the economy of the region for years, but its post-war manifestations were challenging the very soul of the state.

The history of the West and of this region has been one of escape and redemption, people leaving behind one life for a new start. The problem was that the form that redemption took was turning some of the most productive agricultural land in the world into unattractive, very low density, nonfarm sprawl. In the words of former governor Tom McCall, addressing the Oregon legislature in 1973:

> There is a shameless threat to our environment and to the whole quality of life—the unfettered despoiling of the land...Sagebrush subdivisions, coastal condomania, and the ravenous rampage of suburbia in the Willamette Valley all threaten to mock Oregon's status as the environmental model for the nation...the interests of Oregon for today and in the future must be protected from grasping wastrels of the land.

In 1973, after an extensive outreach effort by the governor himself, the legislature passed Senate Bill 100 creating the Oregon Statewide Land Use Planning Program. The 1973 act required that every city and county in the state prepare a comprehensive land use plan, that the plans be prepared to respond to specific statewide land use goals, and that all future land use decisions be made consistent with plans found to be in compliance with the goals.

Zoning codes were specifically directed to implement the comprehensive plans, thereby becoming subservient to the plans. There are three types of goals in the Oregon system. The *process* goals specify how plans are to be developed and how the other goals are to be considered, and they direct that citizen participation be a critical part of the process of plan development and implementation. The *conservation* goals call for the preservation of air and water quality, significant natural and cultural resources, and, most important, farm and forest resource lands. The *development* goals direct jurisdictions to create urban growth boundaries within which urban growth can occur, supported by urban levels of service, in a manner that meets the housing, transportation, and other needs of the community.

In essence, the Oregon system is an agricultural land preservation program that strictly separates urban land use from rural land use. Chief among the reasons the program has been supported three times at the polls, and most recently in our very conservative legislature, is that it maintains farm and forest land for farm and forest uses while creating certainty for those engaged in urban development.

For the metropolitan area, the land use planning program has been extremely important in two ways. First, it has generated a metropolitan urban growth boundary in the Oregon portion of the region, thereby linking the fate of one jurisdiction to another. Second, it has ensured that the 24 cities and 3 counties within the urban growth boundary have all prepared comprehensive plans, with all of those plans prepared according to the same goals, and all incorporating both minimum densities and a requirement for multifamily housing.

In addition to statewide land use planning, the other major policy innovation that has had a significant effect on the urban form of metropolitan Portland was the creation of the Metropolitan Service District, now simply called Metro, in 1979. Metro is a regional unit of government that is directly elected. It has been delegated the task of managing the region's urban growth boundary, thereby controlling the supply of urban land. Although comprehensive land use planning is a task for cities and counties, Metro can require those local plans to change in order for them to be consistent with regional plans. Metro is also the metropolitan planning organization for federal transportation planning purposes, and it has been instrumental in developing a constituency for region-wide transportation planning and the development of light rail.

From these experiences we can draw the following lessons. First, the Portland metropolitan area has experienced some but not all of the city-shaping influences felt by other metropolitan areas. Our major city, Portland, was settled early by Pacific Northwest standards, and in service to an agrarian rather than industrial economy. Second, at key points in its development, our metropolitan area received the serendipitous gifts of leaders and city builders, some in the form of physical features, others in the form of leadership and collective action. Third, nature plays an incredibly powerful and central role in the minds of the people who live here. This is consistently supported by public opinion polling and the behavior of voters at the ballot box. Finally, for much of our history we have been an economic and cultural hinterland to the rest of the nation. This, too, has left its mark on our urban landscape in the form of moderate amounts of almost everything, rather than vast tracts dedicated to one or another activity.

Today, however, the region, its ideas about itself, and its role in the world are all changing. The Portland metropolitan area today is home to some 1.62

million people. Our region crosses the Columbia River into Clark County, Washington, and includes a total of six counties. The urban parts of the three principal Oregon counties are home to about 70% of this population, with most of the remaining 30% in Clark County, Washington. We project a population of about 2.1 million in 2015 and about 2.5 million in 2040. Recent rapid population gains suggest that we might realize those projections sooner rather than later.

Within our urban growth boundary there are about 230,000 acres, or about 360 square miles. Our region's landscape is defined by rivers and mountains. Portland sits at the confluence of the Willamette and Columbia rivers. To the west, over the Tualatin Mountains, is the Tualatin Valley and Washington County. Washington County is the fastest growing county in the state, and home to Nike, Intel, and our very own "silicon forest." It includes an area that Joel Garreau has described as an "emerging edge city," though it physically bears little resemblance to Tysons Corner or other edge city archetypes.

To the south and east of Portland is Clackamas County, the site of early suburbanization, Oregon City, and the foothills of the Cascades. Portland itself is almost completely within Multnomah County, home to some 660,000 people and the site for most pre–World War II urbanization. Clark County, Washington, lies to the north, across the Columbia, and is the fastest growing county in Washington State. It is developing according to a different set of policies, a markedly different cultural view of the natural environment and private property rights, and remains linked to the Oregon side of the region via two bridges.

Although both Washington and Clackamas counties are growing extremely fast by Oregon standards, Washington County is fifth in the state in farm gate receipts and Clackamas County is second. Further, despite agriculture and forestry being the two mainstays of the Oregon economy, high-tech employment has recently eclipsed forest and lumber products employment statewide for the first time. We also tend to be a region of small businesses. Today some 30% of the employment is either in firms of four or fewer or among those who are self-employed. In one of our wealthiest suburbs, a recent survey found that 97% of the business licenses were granted to residential addresses.

Although Portland is a city of 460,000, the next largest city has a population of about 74,000. Unlike Phoenix or other fast-growing urban regions, Portland is not surrounded by cities capable of inflicting great damage on the central city. Today, however, no single jurisdiction, including Portland, can get things done unilaterally. Single jurisdictions can stop things, but they cannot achieve their objectives without working collaboratively with others.

Downtown Portland remains that business and cultural heart of the region. Efforts of the city and the business community to revitalize downtown have resulted in it becoming a 24-hour hub of activity. It continues to maintain its share of employment in the region despite a dramatic increase in the amount of class A office space in suburban locations. In addition to being the location best served by transit, it is also the location best served by highways. The mode split coming into downtown for transit is about 35%, with about 10% arriving via foot or bike. Region-wide, however, the auto mode split is about 94%, with transit accounting for only 2 to 3%.

In the late 1980s, despite having planned like no other region in North America, we found ourselves with many of the same dilemmas: increasing traffic congestion, sprawl within the urban growth boundary, and an uncertain sense of the future. Questions began to be raised that challenged our assumptions about urban form, primarily because we lacked any firm set of principles with which we could respond. In early 1989, Metro began the most recent round of regional planning with the creation of the Regional Urban Growth Goals and Objectives (RUGGO), finally adopted in 1991.

Perhaps the most significant result of the RUGGO process was the creation of a regional planning partnership in the region. It was the jurisdictions within the urban growth boundary themselves that called for the next phase of planning, the development of a 50-year vision to put the goals and objectives into motion. The "Region 2040 Project" was developed specifically to add structure to the region's conception of its physical form. Through the planning process the region would:

1. specify the degree of expansion, if any, required of the urban growth boundary and the locations for any future expansions;

2. identify the major components for the regional transportation system, especially transit components and the creation of a regional pedestrian system;

3. identify a hierarchy and system of places, ranging from downtown Portland to existing town centers to regional centers and neighborhoods; and

4. incorporate a system of greenspaces in the urban region, both for purposes of accommodating outdoor recreation and for maintaining the viability of wildlife habitat.

Region 2040 began by assessing the base case, the probable future if nothing was done, and then developed a range of possible alternatives that collectively mapped the "territory" within which the region's desired concept would be found. Alternatives were generated and extensively tested using linked transportation, air quality, and land use allocation models. Extensive public involvement was incorporated in the review of the concepts, the derivation of the preferred alternative, and the adoption of the final 2040 growth concept.

The adopted growth concept called for very little urban growth boundary expansion over the next 50 years, amounting to about 7% of the existing total. It was targeted to parts of the region needing additional urban growth but avoided the use of lands protected for farm and forest use. The transportation system called for additions to the light-rail system backed up by higher expectations for pedestrian trips within and between important regional centers. Each center will likely serve different functions since this region cannot sustain a large number of places that offer the same things. Light rail is intended not so much as a replacement for the automobile, but as a device that allows people to inhabit the region as pedestrians. Finally, a system of greenspaces was identified to separate communities from each other and continue to protect open space resources within the urban area.

Despite what seems to be an unparalleled level of support and collective effort on behalf of regional objectives, there are a number of outstanding issues that will challenge the commitment of Metro and other jurisdictions in the years ahead. First, holding the line on the urban growth boundary is going to be an extremely contentious issue. Most agree that we have plenty of land for all but one category of future land use: single-family detached housing. Although the development industry has so far not prevailed in their effort to secure large and immediate expansions of the boundary, they will not stop trying. Politicians will be tested at every turn, and time will tell whether we have the fortitude to stick with the plan.

Second, our modeling of the transportation system has convinced us of one central fact: simply arranging things intelligently in space is not enough. We cannot achieve our objectives for the transportation system unless people change their use of the transportation system. It's a question of behavior, and therefore a long-term concern with, in this country, an uncertain future.

Finally, urban historian and planner Carl Abbott described the Oregon policymaking style in recent years as moralistic, "interwoven with strong fibers of status quo conservatism." In the classic mold of the early 20th century progressives, our innovations have been designed to preserve the past, rather than to create a future. Our approach to problems has been managerial, and ultimately rationalistic. Abbott goes on to identify three weaknesses in the Oregon style. First, the rationalistic approach to problems is vulnerable to

political partisanship. It requires compromise, something unlikely in a politically polarized environment. Second, the compromises that get struck can
be "undermined and overwhelmed" by self-righteousness simply because
they are compromises and by definition imperfect from anywhere but the
middle. Third, the Oregon approach to governance and policymaking needs
to be learned and relearned, relying on a shared sense of the rules of the game
and the values of the community.

Oregon's growth has historically resulted for the most part from waves of
in-migration, rather than natural increase. In the past, most of the people
coming to Oregon and to the Portland metropolitan area owed their liveli-
hood to some form of employment tied to an economy based on timber and
agricultural production. Hence, the landscape served as a common bond and
provided a common point of reference. Today, our economic growth is due
primarily to activities that are not extensions of the state's natural resource
base. The split between urban and rural interests is perhaps wider than ever.
In some locations, our population is diversifying at a dramatic rate.

The connections among communities and between communities and the
natural environment are undergoing substantial change. Building and maintaining a consensus about the values that bind us together and to this place
represents a challenge that the state has never had to face before, and which
will be crucial to our success. The transition continues and with it comes the
challenge of forming a new and shared perspective on what matters. As Lewis
Mumford said in a 1938 speech to the Portland City Club:

> I have seen a lot of scenery in my life, but I have seen nothing so
> tempting as a home for man than this Oregon Country...You have a
> basis here for civilization on its highest scale, and I am going to ask
> you a question which you may not like. Are you good enough to
> have this country in your possession? Have you got enough intelli-
> gence, imagination, and cooperation among you to make the best use
> of these opportunities?

His question is probably unanswerable, but his challenge remains current
and echoes still in planning and policy discussions throughout the region.
The Portland region today is still one where it is possible to take a day-trip
to the wilderness. Will it be so in 10 years? Will we still care?

Seattle and the Puget Sound

The Puget Sound region represents the urban side of the state of Washington:
King, Pierce, Snohomish, and Kitsap counties have 56% of the state's popu-

lation and 60% of its employment base. While close to 70% of the population lives in western Washington, central and eastern Washington maintain a strong hold on the state's conservative rural politics.

Western Washington has three urbanized areas along the Cascadia Corridor: Bellingham, the Puget Sound region, and Vancouver, Washington. The Puget Sound area holds a concentration of more than 2.7 million people along Cascadia's Main Street, halfway between Portland and Vancouver, British Columbia. This area is a multicentered conurbation squeezed in a narrow band of land between the Sound and the Cascades. Its major centers include, in approximate order of importance, Seattle to the west (19th century origins, now with 520,000 inhabitants), Bellevue to the east (1950s), and Tacoma to the south (19th century). Secondary cores are Renton, Kent, and Federal Way to the south; Everett, Lynnwood, and Edmonds to the north; Bremeton to the west; and Kirkland to the east. It is estimated that this conurbation will grow by 1.5 million by 2020.

Urbanized Puget Sound lies in a 20-mile by 85-mile basin that is constrained by its natural setting in both the east and west directions, but expandable in the north-south corridor. A well-developed freeway system hugs this geography with Interstate 5 as the north-south axis; the Valley Freeway doubling this north-south axis in the growing southern part of the region; Interstate 405 as a loop or beltway linking north, south, and east; Highway 520 and Interstate 90 as the east-west connector; and Highway 99 following the old military road, essentially in the north-south direction, but meandering through the region's flatter lands. While this network supports the existing distribution of population and jobs well, it also encourages growth in areas that are not targeted for it.

In principle, the multiple cores, combined with the current freeway network, provide a strong and workable structure for further development—the region is both decentralized and concentrated enough to sustain growth. The Growth Management Act of 1990–91 intends to build on this structure and to reinforce it with incentives to develop around the existing cores. However, the system exhibits several weaknesses that threaten the future health of the area. One is the propensity for small employment centers to emerge outside of the existing centers. Another is the spread of manufacturing and office development in flat lands along the Duwamish and Green rivers, lands that a decade ago were strictly agricultural. Finally, aggressive housing development in the eastern parts of the region suggests that the Cascade Range may become the only effective barrier to sprawl.

The urban form of the Puget Sound area is a traditional composite of industry (in its broad economic sense), topography, transportation, and local culture. Generally, an abundant land supply and the expansive spirit of the newly arrived pioneers have given the region a sprawling character from the very beginning of the urbanization process. (Until a decade or so ago, it was unthinkable to settle in any form of housing other than a single-family house. And a 6,000 square-foot lot was called "tiny.") Further, the unusual particularities of the natural setting have had a strong impact on where development occurred over the course of the region's history—particularly, Seattle's unique hourglass shape and the great topographical variations in and near the city center. More specifically, the current urban form derives from four distinct periods of development.

The first period, "the Central City," established Seattle as the region's primary center. The city's deep harbor, which first provided a functional outlet for the region's wood products, became an important gateway to Alaska's gold rush. By the time the intercontinental railroad arrived in the early 1890s, Seattle had bypassed Tacoma in both size and economic power—it had more than 300,000 inhabitants in 1920—and had grown in the north-south dimension in the path of least geographical resistance.

The second period, "Early Suburban Shopping Centers," began before World War II, with industrial development taking over the flat lands of the Duwamish River, first just south of Seattle's downtown and then further down toward Renton, following the river's valley and maintaining easy access to the harbor. In this long and skinny city, this pattern of industrial expansion meant that new housing had to go to the north of downtown. After the war, however, the hegemony of Seattle's downtown as the region's unique center subsided. The nation's first shopping mall, Northgate, opened less than 10 miles north of downtown in 1950, followed, a decade or so later, by a southern counterpart, South Center.

The third period, "the Multi-Nucleated Region," marked the full-fledged expansion toward the east and the transformation of the elongated form into a semicircle (see Figure 2). Freeway construction in the late 1950s and 1960s made this trend a reality with the building of north-south Interstate 5, and of Interstate 405 as the oblong connection to Interstate 5. Eastward expansion was first fueled by residential development, while industrial and office development continued growing in the southern direction. It was encouraged by the building of Highway 520 and widening of Interstate 90, respectively. However, as in most other suburban areas of the nation, major retail tread closely behind housing construction on the east side of Lake Washington, followed, in turn, by office development. Within less than two decades, the freeway network had come to serve as the backbone for a dozen or so new retail and employment centers in the region.

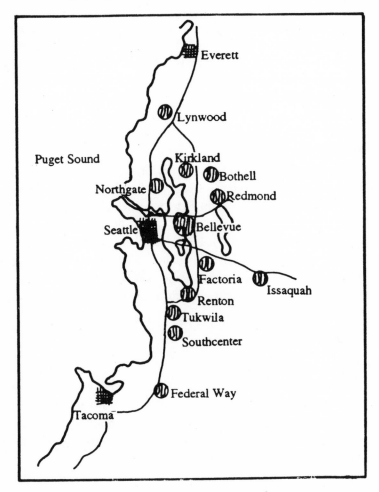

Figure 2. Multi-Nucleation in the Puget Sound Area.

The fourth period brings us to the present, with a newly enacted set of laws regulating growth. The Growth Management Act of 1990–91 is essentially an attempt to maintain the current urban structure, to reinforce existing centers, to take advantage of existing infrastructure, and to prevent further sprawl. The act calls for a boundary to contain new development. It requires the fastest growing jurisdictions to develop comprehensive growth management plans that address transportation, land use, capital facilities, economic development, housing, and utilities. Plans must address these issues together in the way they affect each other. Each city's expenditures must be consistent with the plan—part of a Strategic Capital Investment Plan; plans must be consistent with those of neighboring jurisdictions. Future urban form clearly depends on how successful the region is at enforcing the GMA's mandate.

Eight subject areas best provide the lessons that can be drawn from the Seattle–Puget Sound experience.

Strong Regional Culture

Over the course of its development, the region has benefitted from its relatively homogeneous population—of organized and cooperative people primarily of Northern European extract, with a strong work ethic, and with comparatively little poverty and related social problems. Cultural homogeneity has helped set priorities that are shared and supported by most. For example, as growth began to threaten quality of life, the expected dissension between the rural and urban parts of the state were worked out and the Growth Management Act was passed with relatively little compromise being made.

Location

The isolation of this northwest corner of the United States has been a reinforcing factor in the formation of a regional culture. It has also both forced and allowed the region to develop a broad palette of services and activities, from the major port facilities to the nationally recognized university. Furthermore, the Puget Sound's current position midway between Europe and Asia is an attractive proposition for international trade and will benefit future development.

Activism

Watchdog activity runs high in the region, making any public intervention a challenge. Bottom-up community organizations have always had a strong presence in the political arena. Also important are the several remarkable personalities who have dedicated their lives to causes that have had great effect on the quality of the region. Victor Steinbrueck, an architect and professor at the University of Washington, has been known for first saving Pioneer Square, the 19th century center of Seattle whose function had been taken away by an emerging central business district since the 1930s and 1940s. Steinbrueck then led the fight to preserve the city's public market, Pike Place

Market, which became the first project in the country to use federal urban renewal dollars to preserve a historical setting.

A new breed of activism has emerged recently with the Committee for the Seattle Commons. With several pillars of the community at the lead, this committee has championed the development of a 70-acre park south of downtown in an area currently holding low-intensity downtown services. The park is seen as an essential addition to the current downtown as well as the necessary incubator for the development of a new compact community at the core of the region, and therefore a positive answer to suburban sprawl. If successful, this project will be the first "urban renewal" effort to replace low-intensity development with open space in a highly valuable location. It will also be a test as to whether open space can be a catalyst for development in a city and region where views and water have been the prime movers of real estate.

Leadership

Strong political and business leadership have been instrumental in maintaining Seattle as a viable social and economic community in spite of competitive growth in the region. Jim Ellis, a Seattle attorney, almost single-handedly shaped legislation to clean up Lake Washington and to revitalize the city's recreational and sports facilities in the 1970s. He has also been a steady force in protecting the viability of Seattle's downtown over the past several decades. The current mayor, Norm Rice, has skillfully maneuvered to enhance the city's unique attributes to keep it as an attractive alternative to the suburbs for both residents and businesses.

Physical Geography and Environment

The proximity to the "great outdoors" has been an important asset to the region. Together with comparatively low land prices, it has been the chief instrument for the in-migration from California and has supported an increasingly important tourist industry. The diverse and attractive landscape has saved businesses and industries untold numbers of dollars in allowing them to pay relatively low salaries. However, the so-called "Rainier factor" is a delicate proposition that still pitches businesses against environmentalists. Awareness is only slowly growing that it is an integral part of the economy— for instance, the extinction of a number of salmon species has been a vehicle for discussion of the importance of tourism and specifically recreational fishing in the region.

Timing and Serendipity

A contemporary view of the region tells us that slow, yet sustained development creates settings that can better learn and sense future opportunities. Having California as a precedent is a powerful potion for the people in the Puget Sound area. Because they can actually see and experience what might happen to them, they fear the "Los Angelization" process, resist rapid change, and take time to ponder their future. The region has clearly been cashing in on the California "debacle"—it certainly has been at the root of the growth management efforts and has helped to project better options. Whether the people of the region and the state are actually able to implement a better future remains to be seen.

Secondly, the region has been lucky to be home for key industries at peak times of national and international demand and productivity. Aviation and the related defense manufacturing have helped since the 1940s, particularly through the 1960s. More recently, a large concentration of computer and communication industries have been instrumental in expanding the economy, effectively allowing the region to avoid the recessions that have plagued other parts of the country.

The region prides itself on its attractive physical environment, humane setting, and vital economy. The people of the Puget Sound think of themselves as health- and environment-conscious, well-educated, and compassionate. There is a certain self-righteousness to this attitude and a certain amount of naiveté and provincialism when relating it to the context of the world today. Nonetheless, and given future maturing, the people of the Puget Sound offer all of the right ingredients for the making of good world citizens.

The Seattle Comprehensive Plan, which has been entitled *Toward a Sustainable Seattle,* is structured on three basic principles, social equity, economic security, and environmental stewardship, which summarize well the goals established for the future of the urbanized part of the state. Yet, fulfilling these principles may be difficult if the following issues are not attended to in the near future.

Transportation

The region has been resisting investment in non-auto-related transportation. A proposed multi-modal, decentralized system was approved overwhelmingly by the Seattle and King County electorate, but rejected by the suburban voters. It is significant that the suburban counties, which will assume most of the future growth and which were clearly favored by the proposal to build a subway system under most of Seattle, refuse to address issues of transportation congestion. Ambivalence exists in the region as to how future growth will be accommodated and how the rampant enmity between urban and suburban communities will be abated.

Urban Centers and Villages

The Growth Management Act requires counties and municipalities to develop comprehensive plans based on infrastructure concurrency and to address issues of overlaps between the different jurisdictions. While the act clearly is an excellent first step in addressing growth in a coordinated fashion, the effectiveness of the comprehensive plans in guiding actual implementation of growth policies remains a question. First of all, the growth boundaries are being challenged by those communities that are directly affected, in spite of the fact that they provide more than a 20-year supply of land according to relatively lax standards of development. So the imposition of the new culture of growth boundaries is being aggressively resisted, threatening to substantially weaken efforts to contain growth.

The second major element of comprehensive planning is the consolidation of existing urban centers. These centers, or urban villages as the city of Seattle calls them, aim to be integrated mixed-use urban or suburban cores building on existing infrastructure and services, and thus facilitating a transit-supportive transportation system through densification. Yet the consolidation of these urban centers will not take place without major changes in both the zoning laws currently in place and in the allocation of services within counties and cities. Most cities, and especially the suburban ones, currently have an inordinately high supply of commercial land disseminated erratically within their boundaries. Similarly, multifamily zones have been established based on political pressures and not on the rational integration of housing and commercial services. As a result, in most places, commercial development is spreading, not concentrating, and dense multifamily development is taking place away from commercial areas.

In brief, while we can safely predict that growth and densification will take place in the Puget Sound area, it is not possible to anticipate at this point whether this growth will yield integrated mixed-use cores or whether the urban boundary will remain. Most likely, further "Los Angelization" of the urbanized region will take place along with further consolidation of urban villages, principally in the Seattle area. This mixed scenario also will be influenced by whether or not the concept of "Cascadia" evolves into an economic and physical reality: realizing the Vancouver (BC)–Portland or Eugene corridor will help resolve some of the issues related to international trade with Asia as well as provide opportunities to access a broader range of services without having to duplicate them within each major urbanized area.

The Puget Sound area does seem to deserve the positive reputation that it currently holds nationally and internationally. Its economic vitality and social cohesiveness, combined with a diverse and attractive physical setting, offer a rich and pleasant environment for living. The comparatively slow but steady development of the urbanized region, strong leadership, and grassroots activism all have contributed positively to making it a desirable place to live and work.

The substantial growth projected into the next millennium represents both an opportunity and a threat to the region's future quality of life. Containing further sprawl, consolidating existing land uses, and building on existing infrastructure are the principal challenges ahead, with transportation and capital budgeting for public services as key elements.

Vancouver

Vancouver is the central city in a Greater Vancouver Metropolitan Region of 1.8 million people. The city and the region have experienced very high rates of growth for several decades, and this growth has been accompanied by far-reaching transformational processes, including economic and social change (restructuring), the reshaping of metropolitan space (reconfiguration), and new trading and social–cultural relationships (reorientation). The impacts of these changes upon the natural environment have led to growth management as a key planning priority both at the metropolitan region level and at the local government level.

Vancouver is know as the most scenic city in Canada. Its residents live on a peninsula in the southwest corner of the province of British Columbia, and the region's southern border is shared with the state of Washington. The surrounding waterways—the Burrard Inlet, the Straits of Georgia, and the Fraser River—provide, respectively, a sheltered deep-sea port, convenient access to the Pacific Ocean, and an easy route to the rich agricultural lands of the Fraser Valley and the interior of the province. The city is built on hills with mountains in its backyard and the ocean in its front yard. It has clean air, pleasant temperatures year-round, flowers and sculptured shrubbery every-where, and a livable built environment. Vancouver provides Canada's Asian connections and combines the best features of Los Angeles and San Francisco.

For most Canadians, Vancouver is Canada's West Coast metropolis, but until recently, its status as a Canadian metropolis was granted largely on the strength of its location and size; few would have ever compared it to Toronto or Montreal. Developments since the 1960s have begun to attract interest from the rest of Canada and abroad. Millions of visitors attended Expo '86. Vancouver is acquiring a reputation for being far more than a scenic city. Like its sister cities in the Cascadia Region, Vancouver reached a watershed in the 1960s and 1970s, and by the time it celebrated its centennial in 1986, the city could reasonably claim to have chosen a destiny that appealed to people everywhere.

For much of the city's history, Vancouver's residents were lulled into feeling that none of their activities could seriously impair the city's natural beauty or its destiny as the country's western metropolis. The city began when the Canadian Pacific Railway chose the tiny settlement of Granville as its West Coast terminus; in April 1886 the provincial legislature incorporated Vancouver. Growth was at first slow, but by the turn of the century Vancouver had displaced the capital city of Victoria as the leading commercial center on the coast. Montreal and Toronto businesses established Pacific Coast branches in Vancouver; coastal steamship companies, including Canadian Pacific Navigation and union steamships, made the city their headquarters, and transoceanic liners docked regularly. The pre-war economic boom expanded markets for such British Columbia products as fish, minerals, and lumber.

The worldwide recession of 1913 and the great war of 1914 to 1918 severely reduced trade and resource development, but by the 1920s growth had resumed and Vancouver replaced Winnipeg as the leading city in western Canada. Cheap ocean transport through the Panama Canal opened new markets for British Columbia's resources, while the province's campaign for freight-rate reduction enabled Vancouver to become a major grain-exporting port. After World War II, it was clear that Vancouver's economic future would be shaped by its function as Canada's Pacific port and as the financial, industrial, and distribution center for the resource-based economy of British Columbia.

Population growth along the West Coast of the United States and the recent growth in trade with the Pacific Rim countries has furthered the growth of Vancouver as an international port. Trade with the Asia-Pacific region sur-passed traffic across the Atlantic in 1982. The trade routes between Canada and Asia are now carrying six times as much cargo as ten years ago.

An indication of Vancouver's function as the decision-making heart of the provincial economy is the presence of the Vancouver stock exchange. Since its establishment in 1907, it has emerged as the only significant financial cen-ter in Canada outside Toronto, Montreal, and Winnipeg. Vancouver is also the head-office center for a wide variety of provincial corporations and the major unions. It is the regional center for national enterprises such as char-tered banks. The city also boasts a busy international airport, a modern light-rail transit system, and good ferry service to points on Vancouver Island and in the United States. A sign of Vancouver's growing international importance was the establishment in the mid-1980s of the B.C. International Commer-cial Arbitration Centre, competing with the world's two dominant arbitration centers in London and Paris.

Vancouver's dependence on the very volatile resource base of British Co-lumbia has given it, until recently, a pronounced pro-business atmosphere. In the "rush for spoils," few in the city worried about the more complex issues surrounding the development of a livable metropolis. By the late 1960s, how-ever, concerns about the direction of the region's development and the qual-ity of life ushered in a new phase in Vancouver's development. The region's landscape—for so long taken for granted—has been shaped (or reshaped) in new, imaginative, and sensitive ways. Among the considerable achievements of the reformers and their supporters was the redevelopment of False Creek and later of Granville Island, the rescue and rejuvenation of Chinatown, and the renewal of Gastown.

The redevelopment of these areas indicated that a new approach was being followed with a view to developing a cityscape to match the splendor and liv-ability of the natural environment. This reshaping of space was matched by major social–cultural reorientation as the city and region became multi-ethnic. Vancouver, like Toronto, was experiencing a major influx of immi-grants, most of them from non-European countries. The influence of these "new Canadians" was soon being felt in all aspects of the city's social, cultural, and economic life. Growing connections with Pacific Rim countries and with Seattle and Portland encouraged a sense of distinctiveness in Vancouver and the sense of independence from central Canada.

Vancouver's prospects for the balance of the 1990s and beyond appear fa-vorable, in light of the city's comparative advantages in industrial structure and market orientation, continuing high levels of investment (both domestic and foreign), well-maintained infrastructure, and high amenity levels. However, more problematic aspects of Vancouver's development can be discerned. These include the consequences of growth, manifested by pressures on vulnerable communities in the metropolitan core especially and by the challenge of reconciling the development of the built environment with maintenance of the natural environment. Rapid growth levels also have significant social implications in terms of community polarization, housing affordability problems, and persistently high unemployment, the latter exacerbated by high levels of immigration that have swelled the metropolitan labor force.

These issues point to a larger reality: that Vancouver's development has pushed to the limit and likely beyond the capacity of conventional planning approaches and systems to respond to dynamics of urban growth and change. To be sure, recently prepared plans for the region represent in some ways a state-of-the-art regional growth management framework. But these plans have been developed within an increasingly inadequate context of governance and jurisdiction and thus are essentially adaptations of a model of physical planning now half a century old.

This model has in some ways served Vancouver well, with a legacy including significant green space, new and expanding town centers, and a rational metropolitan structure. The overriding purpose of recent regional plans has been to cope with the problems of growth, but as Tom Hutton has noted in his study of Vancouver, "the challenge of the 1990s (and impending 21st century) includes, as well, more complex aspects of structural change driven by powerful forces of economic globalization, market integration, telecommunications innovation, and greatly enhanced factor mobility, notably capital, technology and labour." The precise nature of the new planning models that are now being developed both in Vancouver and in the Cascadia Region generally is only now emerging. It is clear, however, that the old way of doing things is no longer accepted, and, at a minimum, the new model will include both development and growth management elements, and it will be predicated on broad community participation. The fact is that Vancouver residents have begun to understand that livable regions don't just happen, they are created by the people who live there.

Epilogue

Carlos Schwantes, in his *The Pacific Northwest; An Interpretive History,* after reviewing the history of settlement in the Northwest identifies a dramatic shift in the role of the region from serving as an economic and cultural hinterland to, at least in its metropolitan areas, selectively becoming a national and international trend-setter. Schwantes comments that:

> The juxtaposition of metropolitan trend-setter and hinterland is, in fact, the defining quality of life in the modern Northwest. The accessibility of the hinterland from metropolitan centers remains the *key* feature of what residents regard as a desirable lifestyle . . . the feeling that in some remote part of the region an unsolved mystery of nature may still await the persistent searcher.

Cascadia today, like metropolitan Vancouver, Seattle, and Portland, is a blend of these key ideas. The idea of Cascadia has only begun to try to reconcile the dictates of being both a leader and a follower. Clearly, much remains to be done in the region both physically and conceptually. Nonetheless, the idea of Cascadia gives the cities and other communities in the Pacific Northwest a new strategic way of viewing their respective roles in an international environment. Whether it is the answer, much less an answer to the requirements of building just and healthy cities, remains to be seen. It is a hopeful place to start, and for that reason alone it merits close attention in the years ahead.

Notes

Cascadia

For an overview of the Cascadia Region, see Alan F.J. Artibise, "Achieving Sustainability in Cascadia: An Emerging Model of Urban Growth Management in the Vancouver-Seattle-Portland Corridor," *in* P.K. Kresl and G. Gappert, eds. *North American Cities and the Global Economy* (Thousand Oaks, CA: Sage, 1995).

Portland

Much has been written about Portland, its history, and its planning. Those interested in pursuing the projects and ideas discussed here in greater detail are directed to the following references:

Abbott, Carl, "Historical Development of the Metropolitan Service District," Metro; May 1991

Abbott, Carl, "Oregon as a Public Policy Innovator." Remarks presented to the Urban Affairs Association Annual Meeting, Portland, Oregon, May 4, 1995.

Abbott, Carl, *Portland: Planning, Politics, and Growth in a Twentieth-Century City* (Lincoln: University of Nebraska Press, 1983).

Abbott, Carl "Settlement Patterns in the Portland Region: A Historical Overview" Metro; January 1994.

Metro, "Region 2040 Public Involvement Report," August 1994.

Metro, "Metro 2040 Growth Concept," December 8, 1994.

Metro, "Region 2040: Recommended Alternative Technical Appendix," September 15, 1994.

Metro, "Concepts for Growth: Report to the Council," June 1994.

Metro, "Regional Urban Growth Goals and Objectives," September 1991.

Mumford, Lewis, "Regional Planning in the Pacific Northwest," Northwest Regional Council, Portland, 1939.

Schwantes, Carlos, *The Pacific Northwest: An Interpretive History* (Lincoln: University of Nebraska Press, 1989).

Seattle

The following references expand on the contemporary issues faced by the city:

City of Seattle, "Seattle's Character," Office of Long-Range Planning, April 1991.

City of Seattle, "Toward a Sustainable Seattle, A Plan for Managing Growth, 1994–2014." Adopted July 25, 1994.

Hamer, John, and Bruce Chapman, "International Seattle: Creating a Globally Competitive Community," Discovery Institute, 1993.

Lawrence, Gary, and Steve Nicholas," Sustainability in Seattle: The Evolution of a Concept." Working paper, Center for Sustainable Communities, Cascadia Community and Environment Institute, College of Architecture and Urban Planning, University of Washington, January 1995.

Moudon, Anne Vernez, Dennis Ryan, Eric Schmidt, and Jack Sidener, "Seattle, Washington," in *Case Studies of Ten Cities*, Environmental Design Administration, U.S. Department of Housing and Urban Development, Office of Policy Development and Research, September 1981.

Sale, Roger, *Seattle, Past to Present* (Seattle: University of Washington Press, 1978).

Vancouver

There are several studies of Vancouver's development that are excellent sources for the issues discussed here:

Artibise, A.F.J., "Canada as an Urban Nation," *Daedalus: Journal of the American Academy of Arts and Sciences*, Vol. 117, No. 4 (Fall 1988), pp. 237–264.

Artibise, A.F.J., J. Seelig, and K. Cameron, "Metropolitan Organization in Greater Vancouver," in D. Phares, ed., *Metropolitan Governance Without Metropolitan Government* (Thousand Oaks, CA: Sage, 1996).

Hutton, T., "Vancouver," *Cities,* Vol. 11, No. 4 (1994), pp. 219–239.

Seelig, M.Y., and A.F.J. Artibise, *From Desolation to Hope: The Pacific Fraser Region in 2010* (Vancouver: School of Community & Regional Planning, University of British Columbia, 1991).

Wynn, G., and T. Oke, eds., *Vancouver and Its Region* (Vancouver: University of B.C. Press, 1992).

Mexico City
and Its Region

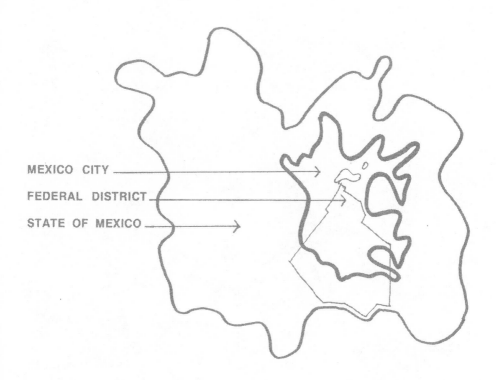

MEXICO CITY

FEDERAL DISTRICT

STATE OF MEXICO

Mexico City is not only the largest city-region in North America, but one of the largest—if not the largest—in the world. Therefore, it displays the problems and possibilities of size, scale, and power in cities. For example, in the 18th century, Mexico City was called "the city of palaces" and "the best jewel in the Spanish crown." Today, unlike major city-regions in the United States and Canada that compete among each other, Mexico City is the political, administrative, commercial, industrial, and financial center of all of its country.

In the opinion of architect-planners Xavier Cortes Rocha and Fernando Greene, who wrote the case study of Mexico City, its size, scale, and power have brought environmental and social problems. It has difficulties with the tensions between the economy, the environment, and social equity; these are readily seen in "overpopulation, environmental pollution, and traffic jams."

Mexico City's issues are manifest in its urban growth and form. While the central areas of the city are mainly dedicated to administrative services and commercial activities, other areas rapidly deteriorate day to day. Because jobs and services are concentrated in three main areas of the city, far away from the residential areas, workers are obliged to make daily long trips, causing traffic problems and air pollution. The territorial distribution of the population, related to their income levels, produces spatial segregation according to economic class. In response to these factors of the economy, environment, and social equity, a joint effort between Mexico City's government and the state of Mexico is currently being developed. Its task will be to plan a metropolitan structure for the future.

Mexico City has pride in itself. In spite of its problems and risks, it seeks to offer much to its inhabitants: "the large capacity for selection between jobs; education and health care at all levels; cultural activities and recreational options; real estate quality, quantity, and variety; as well as social participation." If, indeed, "social interchange is the original reason for cities," then the argument can be made that "Mexico City's richness is not necessarily related to its monetary wealth, but rather to its cultural richness, civic education, social responsibility, and habitability."

Mexico City: The City of Palaces

Xavier Cortes Rocha and Fernando Greene

Mexico City is located in a closed basin, in the geographic center of the country and naturally favored by the richness of its environment and proximity to four highly productive valleys. Before the Spanish conquest six lakes occupied the southern part of the basin, creating an outstanding landscape. However, the city grew over the lakes in a constant effort to keep the city safe from floods. Located in a highly seismic region and punished from time to time by severe earthquakes, Mexico City has had to learn how to build in a safe way, according to the ancient professional wisdom.

After its mythical founding in 1325 and before the arrival of the Spaniards, the city became the capital of a vast empire and reached the dominion of an area that spread out from the coast of the Gulf of Mexico to Guatemala. This was possible because a very sophisticated tributary system allowed the sustentation of a very wealthy and powerful capital city crowded by hundreds of thousands of inhabitants as well as a magnificent surrounding built by the native people. Mexico City has had many ups and downs, nevertheless it has been, almost throughout its history, the most populated city of the North American continent. It was also the imperial capital of the Aztecs. Later on, during the Spanish ruling, it became the center of the viceroyalty, and now it stands as the capital of the Mexican Republic. Moreover, it is the political, administrative, commercial, industrial, and financial center of the whole country.

Prehispanic Time

Chroniclers of the Conquest excitedly described the magnificence and grandeur of Tenochtitlan-Mexico—the way the indigenous city was before

179

the subjugation and destruction performed by the Spanish-led forces. In the Aztec city the main civic-religious center, with its snake-shaped wall, was the highlight of the complex. Outside the core, the city was entirely lacustrine. It had been built with stockades, earth, and stone brought from the surrounding locations. The city was linked to the mainland by four main roads, the widths of which were such that Cortes once wrote about them: "eight horsemen could have walked through them very comfortably." A contention dam separated the salty lakes from the freshwater ones, and it also helped to control the periodic floods that afflicted the city and the growth of the living species in the waters.

Colonial Age

In August 1521, after a long siege by the Spaniards, Tenochtitlan-Mexico was defeated and almost completely demolished. Five months later, Alonso Garcia Bravo, a soldier with knowledge on surveying and a "good geometric," along with Cortes himself, drew the plan for the new city, making use of the preexisting layout.

Mexico City was favored by a privileged situation during the three centuries of the viceroyalty because of the great number of inhabitants and the establishment of the civil, military, and ecclesiastic powers within the city. The viceroyalty's jurisdiction extended from San Francisco to Panama, and from Puerto Rico to the Philippines.

Toward the latter third of the 16th century, the city changed its look from its original austere and defensive aspect to a more open, rich, and ostentatious one. The facades of its buildings were transformed into more cheerful ones, which were opened to an ornamented exterior. The houses began to look like palaces; the churches raised higher up with new building solutions and new decorative styles; and the city became a real metropolis.

During the 18th century, the Century of the Enlightenment, the city magnified and became more beautiful. The baroque style displayed its exuberance in all the buildings, while the cathedral, the finest religious building in all Spanish America, was finished in the purist classical style, with the participation of the masters educated at the Academia de San Carlos (St. Charles Academy), the newly founded Royal Academy of Noble Arts, and the first school of architecture in the New World.

Alexander von Humboldt visited the city and stayed for a long time, comparing it with Berlin and Philadelphia, and concluding that: "its beauty is comparable to other important cities in both worlds with great amounts of big houses, and some of them look small but they are not." He referred to the city as "The City of Palaces." By the time of the Independence, Mexico City was the capital of the best, wealthiest, greatest, most beautiful kingdom in America and, to say it in a few words, the best jewel of the Spanish Crown.

The 19th Century

In 1800 Mexico City had 114,000 inhabitants and it had, among the most important buildings, 36 convents, the University, a theater, 10 schools, 20 boarding houses, and a hotel. Located in the main square of the downtown area was the "Parian," the most important commercial mall of the city. During the first half of the 19th century, the urban pattern and the size of the city did not change; however, the baroque style of architecture gave way to the classical one.

The Federal District was created in 1821, initially having a circular territory with a radius of four leagues and centered in the main square. By 1850 the population had reached nearly 200,000, but the city had a scarce infrastructure. During that year the telegraph was introduced and so was the gas light, both new experiences for the population. Two mule-hauled streetcar lines were established in 1857.

In 1861 President Juarez promulgated a law seizing and nationalizing the properties of the church. In this way, a huge amount of urban land and buildings were introduced into the real estate market, which made it necessary to transform the spatial context of the city with the opening of new streets. Some years later, during the French Intervention, the Avenue of the Empress, now Paseo de la Reforma, was opened, which was and still is the widest and most elegant avenue of the city.

In 1873 the railroad service between Mexico and Veracruz was inaugurated, and various other rail lines began to run, crossing the outskirts of the urban areas and joining the city with all the principal surrounding towns as well as with the northern border towns. Five train stations were built as part of the railway network. The modernization of the country continued, and by the end of the century electric streetcars had taken the place of the animal-traction ones.

The last ten years of the 19th century and the first ten of the 20th century were very intense in regard to the construction of public and private buildings. This construction included the necessary infrastructure as well as urban monuments, according to the industrialization process. At that time the architecture followed the Beaux Art tradition and thus the architects were educated within that School; as a result, the city took on a European shape.

Demographic Growth and Urban Expansion

In 1900 Mexico City had 540,000 inhabitants, which represented 4% of the total population of the country, and by 1910, on the eve of the Revolution, the population had grown to 720,000. During the Revolution (1910–1921), the demographic growth of the country diminished in a considerable way; however, Mexico City not only continued to grow, reaching a population of 900,000 by 1921, but its population growth rate surpassed that of the rest of the country.

Since the 1930s, along with the industrialization process, the city experienced an important population increase and a physical expansion. In 1950 the city reached 3 million inhabitants and had also expanded to the north to the expected limits of the Federal District. As a consequence, the occupation of the contiguous areas of the state of Mexico was begun.

In 1960 the city had 5 million inhabitants; in 1970, 9.2 million; in 1980, 12.37 million; and in the 1990 census the number of inhabitants reached 14.96 million. The constant incorporation of municipalities of the state of Mexico into the metropolitan area of the city eventually resulted in a larger proportion of the city's population residing in the state of Mexico than in the Federal District.

In 1900 the city occupied an urban area of 2,700 hectares (6,750 acres), with a gross density of 200 inhabitants per hectare. Toward 1960 the urbanized surface of the Federal District reached 27,200 ha, (68,000 acres) and was occupied by a population of 4,374,000 inhabitants, a density of about 160 inhabitants per hectare.

By 1970 the urban area of the city was about 38,400 ha (95,000 acres), with the population density of the central city being 222 inhabitants per hectare. Ten years later the area of the city was 75,000 ha, with a population density of 181 inhabitants per hectare. These figures let us know that a suburbanization phenomenon took place during those years and, therefore, the central city reduced its population density. At present, the urban area of the city is estimated to be 87,000 ha (220,000 acres) and has a population density of about 172 inhabitants per hectare (69 per acre).

Urban Government and Administrative Jurisdictions

Until 1950 the urban area of Mexico City was for the most part included within the limits of the Federal District. The city administration depended upon the authority of the city mayor (Jefe del Departamento del Distrito Federal) and 16 delegates under his supervision. As the city overflowed the limits of the Federal District during the 1950s and 1960s, several communities of the municipalities belonging to the state of Mexico joined the city. This situation posed many difficulties, as each municipality had its own government.

At the present time, the metropolitan area of Mexico City includes the Federal District, with its 16 delegations, 26 municipalities of the state of Mexico, and one of the state of Hidalgo. This situation complicates administration of the metropolis enormously, as there are at least 45 authorities, at the local and state level, acting in the metropolitan territory. A Metropolitan Coordination Agency has been established to deal with planning, transportation, and hydraulic issues as an initial mechanism to get these authorities to work jointly, but a major problem is the budgetary difference per capita between the Federal District and the surrounding jurisdictions.

Where the Population Lives and Works

Up until a few decades ago, a very large part of the population lived in the central part of the city. But as a result of the metropolization process, an exodus toward the edge of the city started at the end of the 1940s, due to the enormous number of new neighborhoods being built at that time. Now the central areas are mainly dedicated to administrative services and commercial activities, while other areas remain useless and, consequently, are rapidly deteriorating themselves.

Part of the large migrations directed to the city, beginning in the 1960s, settled in the periphery, especially at the east, and created precarious settlements of great size that were located in flood-prone areas and therefore not suitable for urban development. On the other hand, the industrial zones were located in the center, in the northern part, and to the west of the city. A considerable number of workers are thus obliged to make long daily trips, sometimes of more than two hours, to reach their workplace.

Public and private administration, as well as services, are concentrated in the downtown area and in two other areas: one toward the west (Reforma–Santa Fe) and another one toward the south (Insurgentes). For this reason, employees in these sectors commute from the northwest, east, southwest, and south peripheries to the aforementioned areas, mainly by private cars, causing traffic problems that increase day by day. In spite of communication improvements and new lines of the subway built during recent years, this problem appears to have no near solution.

Urban Layout

Since its founding in 1522 and up to the end of the 1940s, Mexico City's expansion followed a reticular layout, generally keeping its longitudinal direction with a north-south orientation. Beginning in the 1950s, and due to the influence of urban theories adopted from France, England, and the United States, large residential areas located northwest, west, southwest, and south of the city were developed in ways that took into account other layouts—for example, the organic solution and the superblock system. These neighborhoods were developed for the upper middle class and upper classes. The superblock system introduced a new way of organizing the space. However, these systems are not observed in poor neighborhoods, which are constructed following the traditional grid and take up the majority of the area.

Distribution of the Population
According to Income Levels

A study of the territorial distribution of the population based on their income level, carried out in 1992, showed a clear space division of establishment of the families according to their income. The wealthy people and the medium to high classes are located within a "horseshoe-shaped" area that nearly surrounds the city to the west and southwest. The medium class is located to the west of the city, as well as in the central and central-north areas, while the low classes live to the north and east parts of the city.

This phenomenology produces a space segregation among the different classes that live in the city. This separation is more noticeable every day because all the spaces occupied by the more powerful classes are in a continuous privatization process, and hence, large neighborhoods or closed urban areas with controlled access have been appearing. This process is caused partly because of the high criminal index from which wealthy people defend themselves, regardless of the resulting isolation from the rest of the population.

It is thought that in the near future this pattern will not vary. On the contrary, it will prevail and the population's territorial distribution will be clearly defined by incomes; the wealthy and medium to high classes will expand toward the west and south, while the medium to low class grows toward the east and north.

Atmospheric Pollution

During the last few decades, the atmospheric pollution affecting Mexico City has been gradually increasing because of the enormous growth in the number of vehicles, which currently sums to over 3 million and continues to increase at a steady pace. The air pollution increase was also due in part to the fact that until the first half of the 1980s there was an indiscriminate concentration of industries in the city. The city's industrial production represented more than 40% of the whole nation's, while only 20% of the country's population lived in the city. Up until 1985 there was not a strong policy regarding atmospheric pollution of Mexico City. This fact suggests a disturbing future, as the pollution up to this time has been very harmful.

Toward the second half of the 1980s a series of policies were introduced that resulted in 109 specific actions for the Integral Program Against Atmospheric Pollution, which is at present managed by the Metropolitan Commission for the Prevention and Control of Environmental Pollution in the Valley of Mexico. These actions have led to a progressive decrease of the atmospheric pollution level, in spite of increasing fuel consumption.

The main atmospheric pollution constituents are ozone, sulfur oxide, nitrogen oxides, and carbon monoxide; the latter three have been fairly well controlled in the whole city since three years ago, and none of them now exceeds the reasonable annual reference indexes.

Finally, we must say that the program for the improvement of environmental conditions has shown positive results, and in spite of the severe atmospheric pollution problems, the levels have decreased. This is mainly because of the diminishing use of noxious compounds in fuels, the modernization of the Vehicle Verification Program, the replacement of old public transport vehicles, and the use of less polluting technologies in industry.

Morphologic Transformation of the City

Since 1950 Mexico City has increased its physical size considerably, going from a population of 3 million to more than 17 million. In order to be able to attend to the housing and services required, as well as the intraurban movements that are products of this enormous growth, several great constructions have been completed and have transformed the morphology of the city in a considerable way.

First, it is important to mention that since 1950 the transportation system of the city has changed because of the construction of a peripheric highway, an internal ring, and four radials. As part of this project some of the streets and avenues of the central city grid were modernized in order to make traffic flow more efficient. We should also mention that an important effort has been made during the last few years to solve nodal traffic problems with the construction of huge traffic distributors.

Moreover, we should take into account the subway system on which construction was begun during the 1960s and which now gives service to more than 5 million inhabitants per day.

Also, the National Autonomous University of Mexico can be distinguished for its size and unique modern architecture. This campus was inaugurated in 1954 and has been since that date the most important higher educational center in the whole country.

At least ten large housing complexes are important because of their size and their number of inhabitants. These huge concentrations confront severe problems in management, and as a result, nowadays the housing solutions are much smaller.

Also, we should mention the large areas for recreation that existed before the 1950s, such as the first section of Chapultepec Park, and those constructed at the beginning of that decade, called the second and third section of Chapultepec Park; likewise, the Aragón and Xochimilco Parks are very important areas of Mexico City. This latter facility is particularly important because it is the biggest ecological area in the city and because its modernization program included the rescue of more than 90 kilometers (56 miles) of channels of clean water. This project was recognized by the United Nations as one of the most important ecological recoveries of recent times.

Urban Planning

The ancient Mexico City was an extraordinarily well-planned city that would today be called an ecologically self-sustained system.

The Spanish conquerors of the 16th century did not appreciate the characteristics of the native city, and therefore they changed it into one in which the Renaissance utopias developed, as it was generously spacious, well organized, and proud of its role.

The first development plan, designed by the Spanish military engineer Ignacio Castera at the end of the 18th century, had as its main purpose the regularization of the city. As the growth of the city was rather slow during these years, urban planning was not a concern until 1930 when Carlos Contreras, an architect and urbanist, prepared a second master plan.

From that year until the 1970s, many important planning projects were carried out. These were mainly related to the layout of communication services. In 1975 a more holistic perspective was taken, and a very important urban planning team was established in order to analyze all different kinds of issues considered vital to the establishment of a new urban plan. That same year, the Federal District Urban Development Act was approved, followed by the approval of the aforementioned General Development Plan in 1980, which established, for the first time, land use plans for the central city included in the Federal District area.

Nowadays, a joint urban project between the Federal District and the state of Mexico is being developed in order to assure a metropolitan structure for the future. However, it is important to recognize that a megalopolitarian vision is needed because the phenomenology of Mexico City should include the analysis of several large cities built in the surrounding area within 50 to 100 kilometers (30 to 60 miles) of the center city.

Future Challenges

It is estimated that by the year 2010 Mexico City will reach a population of between 22 and 25 million inhabitants. Although this is one of the most conservative estimates, it represents an increase of approximately 8 million people over the present population.

In order to meet this conservative estimate we must continue to reduce the growth rate; hence, it is necessary to constantly double our efforts to maintain family planning educational programs that have resulted in drops in the growth of the annual birth rate from 3.5% to 2% in the last 25 years.

Future growth will also require an additional area of 400 to 500 square kilometers of territory to handle the expected population, 80% of which will be housed in the conurbated municipalities of the state of Mexico since the suitable land within the Federal District area will be filled. This situation will bring an important change in the equilibrium of the two Federative entities, since the majority of the city will then be in the state of Mexico rather than in the Federal District.

Due to all the aforementioned facts and because of the growing complexity in managing the city, it will soon be necessary for one governmental organization to manage the entire metropolitan area.

Future growth also puts pressure on the need to rethink the policy for water supply to the city. Currently 70% of the water is extracted from the subsoil, and due to the soil characteristics this has caused some of the structures in the city to begin sinking. Therefore, in the first place, actions related to the efficiency and/or maximization of preservation and recycling of water should be taken into consideration. Water should also be transported from rivers in the southern part of the country because of their ample water supply.

The continuing growth of Mexico City will also carry a greater amount of pollution. Because of this, it is not only imperative to control the levels of the present emissions of pollutants in the air, but it will also be absolutely necessary to comply with the norms required and to enforce clear and strong policies to make industry and vehicles more efficient so that atmospheric pollution is reduced.

High levels of atmospheric pollution have caused the annual median temperature to rise 2°C during the last 90 years, with 1.1°C of this increase occurring during the last 50 years. This rise in temperature is also partially due to the increase of population, as well, because this has necessitated more paved surfaces (which hold in heat more readily than unpaved areas) and promoted industrial expansion (which contributes to warming of the ambient air) within the urban area.

Conclusion

Mexico City's residents are looking forward to their city becoming an efficient and competitive city in which equipment, services, and facilities, as well as carefully planned and programmed public administrative action, will favor an urban environment in which citizens will be able to live together with dignity. The residents want a clean city where a collective conscience regarding environmental preservation will be strengthened; Mexico City is thus determined to enhance and protect its urban environment as the basis of an economic development and improvement of the quality of life. The vision is of a cultured city with new open spaces for the physical, mental, and spiritual development of its inhabitants.

Needless to say, Mexico City has important advantages, such as the highest level of education in the nation, an abundance of qualified workers, a considerable concentration of enterprise capacity, an efficient base of equipment and services, the nation's best road network, an ample and sophisticated market, and large and attractive tourist facilities. And it is precisely on the basis of these advantages that it is possible to create an economic project for Mexico City that will respect the environment and maintain the demographic equilibrium. This project could make Mexico City a city of excellence and grandeur that will inspire in its inhabitants the pride of belonging to a great community.

Afterword

The United Nations Conference on Human Settlements, Habitat II, was successful in bringing the concept of partnership to the international fora. It will be remembered as the conference of partnerships between and among different actors of the society who have an important role to play in the creation of human settlements and cities. These actors include governments, nongovernmental organizations, local authorities, the private sector, parliamentarians, and academics. With the use of a new concept of a partnership committee, a dialog was established between the government representatives and the partners as never before at United Nations conferences. Mayors for the first time before an international audience made firm commitments to reach the goal of sustainable development of human settlements in their cities.

This United Nations conference brought to a close a series of world conferences designed to define and launch a global agenda to meet the complex challenges created by a century of unparalleled change. The issue of shelter and sustainable human settlements is recognized as a problem of crisis proportions that affects all countries. The crisis appears in stark and dramatic statistics. In the year 2025 the earth is expected to be home to almost 100 mega-cities, each with a population exceeding 5 million. It is hoped that the Habitat II Agenda, the Global Action Plan adopted by the conference, will prepare the ground for a new era focused on partnerships involving states, cities, private sectors, NGOs, the scientific community, and their new competitors for resources and influence in a rapidly globalizing world. The Habitat II Agenda hopes to create essential alliances at the community level.

The Habitat Agenda contains a number of policy innovations that have not been seen in other conferences, including references to the sexual exploitation of young women and children; gender desegregated data collection; prevention of lead poisoning; measures to take account of the social and environmental impact of policies; a strong commitment to the economic improvement of women, with references to right to inheritance and flexible collateral conditions for credit; the affirmation of the right to adequate standard of living for all people and their families; and the need for corporations to become more actively involved in human settlement issues.

Even as this last of the UN conferences of the 20th century concluded its deliberations, debate continued as to whether UN conferences are useful or not. The debate will go on, but it should not cloud the conferences' importance in establishing an international value system that cuts across religious, ethnic, national, and racial boundaries. The conferences have spanned some of the most serious and pressing challenges that will confront the world community in the next century, and they have provided us with a more holistic, humane message about our global problems and about the cooperative solutions they require—solutions that all came home at Habitat II. It is a message that we hope will now provide the political will and action to improve living conditions all over the world.

ALIYE PEKIN CELIK

Index

191